DEDICATION

This book is dedicated to the eight people whom
I have loved and who have loved me and
inspired me along my life's journey, then and
now: my mother and father, my maternal
grandmother and grandfather, my brothers
Richie and Randy, my dear wife and soulmate
Michele, and my dear daughter Lindsay.

D1564658

Contents

3

INTRODUCTION

Picture a scene of the perfect vacation or the perfect family weekend getaway. It was a very warm, summer-like afternoon. There was a long pristine lake running north-to-south, spotted with tree-filled islands, as well as several rowboats and sailboats. On the east side of the lake there was an inlet with a small sandy beach. Next to the inlet was a large swimming pool resembling an amphitheater, the pool being semi-circular with a large water fountain in the middle, splashing water on a lot of happy kids. While the east side of the pool had the beach, the north side had wooden bleachers set up crescent-shape, with beach chairs and mounds of sand for sitting and relaxing. South of the pool was a concession area with a large cafeteria and several small shops. West of the pool was a heavily wooded area with a dirt path for hiking. Curiously, there was no sign of any motor vehicles or even parking areas.

The above scenario is an actual dream I had one night several years ago. It could also represent the first five or six years of my life. While many specific moments of those first few years are somewhat vague due to the passage of time, I have enough memories of those early years to conclude that they were the happiest, or at least the most serene and stress-free, of my life.

WINTER – 1954

The early morning hours of January 15, 1954 were cold and windy with heavy snow falling. Low visibility made driving difficult, but my father managed to make his way to North Shore University Hospital in Manhasset, Long Island, where Robert Kenneth Altman was born at 4:05am, the first child of Joseph and Norma Altman. To put this date in perspective, Dwight D. Eisenhower was President of the United States, the polio vaccine was beginning to be tested on children, "Oh My Papa" by Eddie Fisher was the number one song on The Hit Parade, and a day earlier Marilyn Monroe and Joe DiMaggio were married.

My father, Joseph Albert Altman, grew up in the East New York section of Brooklyn, while my mother, Norma Altman (nee Rosenzweig) was raised in the Bronx. My parents met in Rockaway, Queens. My dad shared an apartment there with some buddies a few years after his discharge from the Army. My mom was sharing an apartment with some girlfriends. They were married on June 24, 1951 and went to Niagara Falls for their honeymoon. My dad, holding a college degree in Engineering, got a job as a tool-designer at Waldes-Kohinoor in Long Island City, Queens, a company specializing in the design, sales, and distribution of retaining rings, fasteners that hold components or assemblies onto a shaft.

My parents wanted to start a family and my dad preferred to live in some proximity to his job. My mom had no siblings and wanted to live close to her parents, Michael and Elsie Rosenzweig. They decided to purchase a co-op in a new apartment complex called Hilltop Village, located in Holliswood, Queens. Hilltop was a complex made up almost entirely of young Jewish middle-class couples looking to start families in the Post-World War II era. It consisted of nine 6-story buildings: the Alpine, the Belmont, the Cumberland, the Dover, the Everest, the Fairmont, the Greenwood, the Hampshire, and the Ivy Ridge. Each building had an A-Wing and a B-Wing, and each wing had a basement with a laundry room, bicycle room, storage room, and incinerator room, as garbage was burned at that time. A superintendent, or "super," was assigned to each building. There were four playgrounds scattered throughout Hilltop, including one behind the Dover. The Dover building was the original model for the complex and was different from the other buildings in that you had to go outside to get from one wing to the other. My parents purchased an apartment in the B-Wing of the Dover building, Apt. B45 (87-15 204th Street.) Wanting to be near their daughter, my maternal grandparents moved into a 3-story apartment complex across Francis Lewis Boulevard called Cunningham Heights.

Francis Lewis Boulevard was the main thoroughfare adjacent to Hilltop, running north-to-south from Whitestone to Laurelton. It's surface near Hilltop was cobblestone, making for a bumpy car ride. In the early 1960's the cobblestones were removed and replaced by asphalt.

SPRING 1954 – WINTER 1955

My life as an infant was typical. My mom took me in my carriage to the Dover playground where she hung out with the other mothers. My grandparents took me to parks around their neighborhood. The Dover playground was a good representation of a 1950's playground, with a sliding pond, swings, a see-saw, and a sandbox which for some reason was quickly removed.

8

Once I began walking I was able to make full use of the playground's amenities while my mom sat on the green-painted wooden benches, talking with other moms while keeping an eye on me. As the ground was concrete, our moms always had to be cognizant of our location to insure we wouldn't fall and hurt ourselves. There was a little girl in my building named Rochelle, with whom I often played with. My other early friends included Joanne and David Panzer, a sister and older brother who lived two doors down from me in Apt. B43.

In addition to the Dover playground and the parks near my grandparents, I played in McLaughlin Park, located a few blocks north of Hilltop near the Grand Central Parkway. McLaughlin Park was often called "Little Cunningham Park" due to its close proximity to the much larger and well-known Cunningham Park. It had multiple swings and sliding ponds, as well as a sandbox which I frequently played in.

Grocery shopping was usually done at one of two supermarkets at our local strip mall on Hillside Avenue. The larger supermarket was called Sunrise (later changed to Grand Union,) and the other store at the far end of the strip mall was Bohack, with its smooth, cream-colored outside walls.

SPRING & SUMMER – 1955

In 1955 I had my first airplane ride as I went with my parents to California to see my paternal grandparents. My dad's father, Max, left his family in Brooklyn in 1938 when my dad and his older sister Evelyn were young, and started a burglar-alarm business in the Los Angeles area. My dad's mom, Fanny Horn, died before I was born, and Max remarried a woman named Bess. Unlike my maternal grandparents, who were very warm and personable, Max was kind of aloof, with a thick Austrian accent. We stayed at Max and Bess' home in Alhambra, a suburb of Los Angeles. Around this time Disneyland had its grand opening. I thought my parents had taken me there, but my dad said we were in California just prior to its opening.

FALL 1955 – FALL 1957

Back in Hilltop I spent the next couple of years playing with my parents, grandparents, and friends. I have vague memories of my toddler years: my parents, grandparents, and I playing "Ring-Around-the-Rosie," "The Hokey-Pokey," and "London Bridges Falling Down" and reciting nursery rhymes. Some songs from the 1950's and early 1960's trigger memories for me. I remember hearing Doris Day's "Que Sera Sera" as I went with my mom to the candy store, and Les Baxter's "The Poor People of Paris," heard while playing in McLaughlin Park. I recall sitting on a park bench in Cunningham Heights with my grandmother as Percy Faith's "Theme from 'A Summer Place'" played on someone's radio. Songs by Perry Como, Patti Page, Nat "King" Cole, and The McGuire Sisters were on the radio, both at home and in stores. Music was important to my parents, and my mom sang many songs to me, such as "Getting to Know You," "A Bushel and a Peck," and "Mairzy-Doats." My dad liked to sing the old song "Dry Bones" to me as I sat on his lap. I had a children's album by Danny Kaye which I listened to over and over, especially enjoying the song, "Mommy, Give Me a Drink of Water."

As with many 1950's households we had a large wooden console in the living room. There was a black-and-white TV in the middle, with a liquor cabinet on one side and a magazine/bookshelf on the other. My TV viewing consisted of cartoons, puppet shows, and other shows geared towards young children. TV was still in its infancy and most children's shows at that time were done live and in New York City. My early TV viewing included Howdy Doody, Kukla Fran & Ollie, Bozo the Clown, Romper Room (remember "do-bee," "don't bee," and the "magic mirror,") and of course, the Mickey Mouse Club. Before each show I put on my

11

Mickey Mouse ears and sang the closing theme song along with my fellow mouseketeers. I thought Karen was the cutest, but of course I also loved Annette. One day my parents took me to Manhattan where I met the host of the Mickey Mouse Club, Jimmie Dodd. I had a long-playing album as well as several yellow and orange-colored 78-RPMS with songs from the Mickey Mouse Club and other Disney shows. My parents probably got a kick out of seeing a 3 or 4-year-old boy singing and dancing in the living room to Mickey Mouse records!

When I was three years old my parents took me to see my first movie. I think it was the re-release of "Cinderella," although I have vague memories of seeing the movie version of "Oklahoma" at a very early age. During the next few years they took me to see the movies "Snow White and the Seven Dwarfs," "Sleeping Beauty," "South Pacific," and the original version of "The Shaggy Dog."

WINTER – 1958

In early 1958, as I had just turned four-years-old, we got a new addition to our family: Richard Fred Altman was born on February 21, 1958. Rather than being jealous of the attention my new baby brother was getting, I loved Richie instantly, maybe seeing him as a new toy to play with. I helped my mom feed him and bathe him and I played with him when he was in his crib or the wooden playpen set up for him in the living room. Richie was born with his feet slightly misaligned; this was quickly corrected by shoes with a metal bar connecting the front of them. I was also born with my feet sticking out a little. Curiously, nothing was done to correct my feet, though I've managed to live with this slight deformity.

During my early years I saw a lot of my extended family. Although my mom was an only child my grandmother had many siblings, several of them living at the time in Brighton Beach, Brooklyn. There were Aunt Dinah and Uncle Murray and their daughter, Barbara. Uncle Murray had a big moustache, smoked a cigar, and was very friendly. There were Aunt Shirley and Uncle Meyer and their daughter, Phyllis. Aunt Shirley was always bright-eyed, cheerful, and smiling, and Phyllis was very pretty and would soon get divorced from her husband, Bob. There were Aunt Jean, who was in a wheelchair due to multiple sclerosis, and Uncle Dave and their son Henry, a future attorney. I remember visiting Aunt Dinah and Uncle Murray in Brooklyn and seeing tenement-like apartments with clothes hanging on outside clotheslines; they were apparently less than affluent. My relatives also visited us at our apartment, with Uncle Murray

13

and Uncle Meyer spending lots of time around the liquor cabinet. I was always excited when my aunts and uncles came over. They were very kind to me and paid me a lot of attention. Their kindness and generosity always made me feel important.

My father's relatives consisted of his older sister, Evelyn, and her husband, Meyer Wiener. They had two daughters, Joyce and Sharon, and lived in Brooklyn, off of Pennsylvania Avenue. The Wiener family were decent people, but they were kind of fuddy-duddies. I was never happy when I saw my dad driving onto the Interboro Parkway going from Queens to Brooklyn because I knew we were visiting them. My cousin Joyce was older, not very attractive, and always tried to kiss my brothers and I. Sharon was a few months older than me, not unattractive, but a little slow. My dad also had an Aunt Hattie, who lived in Jamaica with his Uncle Al. I didn't like visiting her because she always kissed us and pinched our cheeks, but I did appreciate the dollar bill she gave each of us at every visit. I much preferred the company of my mom's relatives to those of my dad's.

Being four years old I was unaware of current world events. That being said, I do have a vague recollection of watching TV and seeing Elvis Presley being inducted into the Army. I recall seeing him in a barber's chair, having his hair cut off. I also vaguely recall a satellite being sent into space, and President Eisenhower making speeches. I also remember having my tonsils out. My parents read me a book about what to expect when you go to the hospital. Their promises of lots of ice cream and ices after the operation made me feel a little better. I remember being in the hospital prior to the operation, my dad saying goodnight to me as he closed a curtain around my bed. I can recall the sore throats in the following days and was pleased that my parents came through on their promise of daily doses of ice cream, ices, and sherbet.

<u>SPRING 1958 – FALL 1958</u>

I believe it was the spring or summer of 1958 when my mom and I went with Joanne and David as their mother Nora drove us to the Aquacade at the Flushing Meadow Park Amphitheater to see a performance which included synchronized swimming and other aquatic-themed events. The amphitheater was around a long time, having been a holdover from the 1939-1940 New York World's Fair. Although my memory has faded somewhat, I remember enjoying the show very much. The song "26 Miles" by The Four Preps brings back memories of that day. I also remember going to Madison

15

Square Garden to see the Ringling Brothers and Barnum & Bailey Circus. While one would think I'd enjoy the circus, I was bothered by what I perceived as mistreatment of the animals. For instance, I didn't like the lion-tamer constantly whipping the lions in the face. Even at a young age I felt an empathy and compassion for animals.

Lake George, located in upstate New York, was really the first time I was exposed to a country-like environment with trees, birds, flowers, lakes, and mountains. I spent a couple of weeks in the summer of 1958, as well as 1959, at a bungalow colony there, with my parents, grandparents, and Richie. I had a nice time splashing around in the lake and trying to catch fish. I also became creative, like seeing how many chairs in a row I could line up. There was a swing set there and other children to play with. There was a nice man there whom we called "Whitey" because he always wore a white t-shirt. Across the other side of the lake and bordering on Lake Champlain was Fort Ticonderoga, an old fortress utilized during the American Revolution. As my dad loved military history, we went on a ship across the lake to the fort, where we observed the cannons and visited an adjacent military museum. I recall being very frightened when the ship took off, as the sound of its horn was deafening. Nearby Lake George was a place called Storytown USA, an amusement park with a Mother Goose theme. I talked with Little Bo Peep, watched Jack and Jill go up the hill, and saw Jonah and the Whale. I went on some rides and had a great time.

16

Overall, those few weeks at Lake George were an exciting and enjoyable experience.

WINTER 1959 – SUMMER 1959

By 1959 I was beginning to focus more on friendships. Mark Levine was essentially my best friend growing up, even though our friendship became somewhat contentious in later years. Mark was the only child of Seymour and Toby. He lived on the 2nd floor of the B-Wing, later moving to the 5th floor of the A-Wing. His maternal grandmother, whom he called "Nana," lived on the 1st floor B-Wing and owned some parakeets. Mark and I seemed to enjoy the same toys and games and we played well together. My friends and I used to call him "Marky Maypo" after the Maypo hot-cereal commercials. In 1957 or 1958 our moms took us to Manhattan to see a live taping of "Time for Fun," a children's show starring Bill Britten as a character named "Johnny Jellybean." Mark and I sat in the audience with the other children as Mr. Britten entertained us with comedy skits, puppetry, and magic tricks.

In 1959 things changed. First, the Panzers' left Hilltop and moved to Maryland. My parents wanted a larger residence, so we moved into their old apartment, B43. Mr. & Mrs. Wolf, an older couple, moved into our old apartment. Our new place had two bedrooms; my parents took the larger bedroom while I shared the smaller bedroom with Richie, who was still in a crib.

The most shocking thing that happened in 1959 involved my maternal grandfather. My grandfather Michael, or Mike, was a typical blue-collar-working New Yorker with street-smarts and a Brooklyn accent. It seemed like he was always either smoking a pipe or chomping on a cigar. His one claim to fame occurred in 1959 when his picture was in the newspaper! He had been shot in the leg, as a bullet from a police shootout ricocheted off an object and became embedded in him. Fortunately, he made a full recovery.

My grandfather worked as a bus mechanic for the New York City Transit Authority. For him to get to work he had to take a bus from his apartment in Cunningham Heights to 179th Street and Hillside Avenue, then take the subway into Manhattan. To make the commute easier my grandparents moved into a small first-floor apartment on 164th Street in Jamaica; now my grandfather only had to take a train to work.

With Joanne and David gone I found other kids to play with, mostly from the Dover building. In addition to Mark Levine, the A-Wing had Eddie Wolkis and his younger brother, Stevie. Eddie and Stevie both had freckles and had reddish hair like their mom. Their parents, Bernice and Phillip, were always very nice to me. As I walked into the front entrance of the Dover I often saw their mom through her third-floor kitchen window, her bright red hair being very prominent.

Other friends included Kenny Schneider, who had an older brother as well as a younger brother, Woody. One floor up from me in the B-Wing was Marvin Berk, who became one of my best friends despite being a jerk and a troublemaker. On the first floor was Sammy Gische. Sammy walked with a slight limp due to a mild case of cerebral palsy. He and I became good friends. I remember as a little boy playing with toy soldiers in the room he shared with his older sister Joyce. There were some other kids in the Dover who moved away within a few years, such as Steven Alberti, Kenny Moliver, and Joanne Solomon, who moved out to Oceanside, Long Island in the early 1960's. Some older kids in the Dover B-Wing included Steve Finkelman and Gary Gershoff, and in the A-Wing were sisters Maxine and Linda. Directly above my apartment were Ellen Baras and her older sister Muriel. I also had a friend in the Cumberland named Barry Asrelsky, who attended one of my birthday parties in my apartment.

Although most of our birthday parties were celebrated in our respective apartments, the Dover social room provided an occasional site for them, which included the requisite pizza, soda, and birthday cake, and games like "Musical Chairs" and "Pin the Tail on the Donkey."

Almost all the neighbors I knew in the building were very nice. Next door to me in Apt. B44 was Ruth Schneider. Mrs. Schneider had a red-haired daughter named Lois, who was a few years older than me and once came over to play Candy Land with us. Two floors below me was Carol Prowler, her husband, and son, Steven, who was nasty and stuck-up. Every weekday around 6pm I heard a distinctive whistling outside my window; it was Mr. Prowler coming home from work and letting Carol know he was home and it was time to put up dinner.

At five-years-old I was a typical rambunctious boy. I played a lot in the Dover Playground as my mom sat on the benches with Richie in a carriage or stroller. My friends and I played the usual children's games like "tag" and "hide-and-seek," as well as inventing our own weird games such as "lick-the-eye," a game similar to giving someone a wet-willy. We used thick pieces of chalk to draw a path on the ground which we then followed by riding on our tricycles. I once had an unfortunate mishap as I fell off my tricycle, causing blackening on one of my front teeth; fortunately, it was a baby tooth and it was extracted a couple of years later.

We used to tease some of the girls from the other buildings as they were playing jacks, jumping rope, playing hopscotch, or bouncing rubber balls under their leg ("A my name is Alice.") The boys and girls would throw childish expressions at each other, like "Baby, baby, stick your head in gravy" and "That's so funny I

20

forgot to laugh." The boys were more troublesome than the girls as we would run around the grass in front of the buildings. Hilltop had hired a few private police officers to patrol their streets. With crime being at a minimum it seemed their only job was to chase us off the grass, warning us of serious consequences if we went back on. We also played with hula-hoops, cap-guns, and had metal roller-skates which we put on over our shoes to skate around the outside of the Dover. There was a metal railing in front of the entrance to the Dover B-Wing. Mark pretended to be a train engineer as he sat on the front of the railing pulling on a chain as we lined up behind him on the railing. As long as the weather cooperated, life as a young child in Hilltop was carefree and fun.

I was fortunate to be a healthy child, only experiencing the usual childhood illnesses of chicken pox, mumps, and German measles. However, at around five-years-old I did have a very bad case of the measles. I was ill and in bed for several weeks, feeling very weak and feverish. I was forced to take this awful-tasting, chalky medicine. I still get a bad taste in my mouth when thinking back to that foul-tasting medication. Fortunately I made a full recovery. As with other children at that time I was vaccinated against polio, giving my parents and I one less concern.

Later in 1959 I attended Creative nursery school. I recall playing in various parks and playgrounds and going on the merry-go-round in Valley Stream State Park. The leader was named "Eddie Spaghetti," and I remember having a good time, despite missing my usual playmates.

FALL – 1959

In September 1959 I began kindergarten at P.S. 135, which was located about five blocks away in Queens Village. That first day my mom walked me to school and introduced me to my teacher, Mrs. Sanders. Kindergarten was half-days in the mornings and mostly involved arts and crafts, playing with blocks, finger-painting, and learning a few letters and numbers. There was a small playground right outside the door which my classmates and I frequently utilized. My mom took me home from school about noontime, and I got home just in time to watch a live TV program aimed at young children called "Fun at One."

Although these early years may seem idyllic (except for the measles), don't be fooled by this. My happiness was somewhat tainted as I suffered from a chronic, low-grade depression, along with public anxiety, both of which continued into adulthood. Experts refer to these conditions as "Social Anxiety Disorder (S.A.D.)" or "Selective Mutism," situations where social interactions and speaking in public cause irrational anxiety. I was very shy and introverted, very gullible and sensitive to criticism and ridicule. As my mom walked me back and forth to school, I walked with my head down. When classmates said hello to me in the street, I ignored them. Sometimes my mom got angry at my behavior and gave me a smack in the head, which only helped to humiliate me and make matters worse. I was also sucking my thumb, both in public and in private, which I continued to do throughout childhood. I'm not quite sure why I was so depressed and insecure. It may have been partially hereditary as my mom displayed occasional signs of depression.

Most young kids are sensitive, but my case was more extreme. I spent all of kindergarten without speaking one word to the teacher or to classmates. There's one instance I remember well: we all made these little umbrellas out of balsa wood, covering them with orange construction paper. One by one the students went up to the teacher and told her what colors and decorations they wanted on their umbrella. When the teacher asked me what I wanted I refused to speak up. As a result, I was the only student who went home with a plain-looking umbrella. I was outgoing and talkative at home and with close friends, but for some reason interacting with new kids and new authority figures really scared me to death, so I kept my head down and didn't talk.

The periodic "Show-And-Tells" were especially uncomfortable for me. I only recall participating one time: I brought in a "multi-game" board. Fortunately the teacher, rather than me, explained most of its details to the class.

My depression, over-sensitivity, gullibility, lack of self-esteem, and fear of strangers continued throughout childhood, negatively impacting my ability to fully enjoy and embrace those early years. Kids who are very shy and withdrawn are often targets for ridicule and bullying from other kids and I was no exception. Whatever kids would label me, I tended to believe. For instance, I was called names like "stupid," "retarded," "sissy," "ugly," and "idiot," and I figured they knew what they were talking about. Sometimes when I was allegedly misbehaving my mom or dad would smack me, saying something like "Are you stupid?" and I'd think to myself, "Yes, of course I am!" When they got angry at me, my parents and grandparents would sometimes blurt out hurtful things, like "You lousy good-for-nothing!" (I really hated that one.)

As I went on through grade school some of my negative emotions lessened. However, I unfortunately replaced some of my bad behaviors with others, as I began acting inappropriately in my classes due to a misguided desire for attention. Again, the biggest challenge I had as a child was overcoming my depression and the bad behavior that goes with it, but at the same time not replacing it with other equally negative behaviors.

My depression would lessen at times, like when I found exciting activities to get involved with. My dad was a big football fan. He loved college football and would often sing their fight songs to me. He was also a New York Giants fan, and in 1959 he took me to a Giants game at Yankee Stadium. Frank Gifford, #16, was the biggest star of the team, and I remember wanting to send him a get-well card when he was hospitalized with an injury. A few years later my dad took me to a New York Titans football game at the Polo Grounds in Manhattan (the Titans would become the New York Jets a few years later.) I would not become a sports fan for several more years, but it was exciting going to the games and having my dad explain all the action to me.

WINTER & SPRING 1960

As 1960 began and I turned six-years-old, my parents took me to see the movies "Toby Tyler" and "The Three Worlds of Gulliver." I also made some visits to the dentist. Dr. Grossman was an older gentleman who had a practice in the Bronx. I'm not sure why he was our dentist; perhaps my mom or grandparents knew of him. As the Throgs Neck Bridge connecting Queens with the Bronx was not yet built, we took the Grand Central Parkway to the Triboro Bridge, then took a smaller bridge (which I called "the long long bridge") to his office. He had a rather dingy first

25

floor office in an old apartment building. Curiously he stayed in the exam room while taking X-rays, not taken any precautions against radiation. At the end of our visits he always gave us a bag of pretzel nuggets. We stayed with Dr. Grossman for a few years, then wisely switched to dentists closer to home, Dr. Green in the Cumberland and Dr. Singer on Hillside Avenue.

As the weather got warmer my parents took Richie and I on some nice outings. We went to a place called Lollipop Farm in Syosset, Long Island. Lollipop Farm was basically a petting zoo where kids would pet lambs, feed ducks, or ride on their signature attraction, a small gasoline-powered train that wound through the property. I remember being frightened when a duck snapped at me. We also made a few visits to the then very popular Freedomland, an American History-themed amusement park located in the northern part of the Bronx. Freedomland consisted of several themed sections, each representing a location and era of American History. There were horse-and-carriage rides, trolley rides, and western re-enactments, to name a few. It was not unlike Disneyland. I was saddened when Freedomland closed in 1964, later to be replaced by a high-rise apartment complex called Co-Op City.

The amusement park I visited the most was Kiddy City, located only a few miles away from us on Northern Boulevard in Douglaston. It was a small amusement park, but I loved the roller-coaster, spook house, bumper-cars, and the adjacent miniature golf course. It seemed every time I went there I ran into friends and fellow Hilltoppers. Sadly, in the mid-sixties a fire destroyed some of the park, and it eventually went out of business, later replaced by a successful golf driving-range.

While we enjoyed playing in the Dover playground and McLaughlin Park, my parents took us to some other playgrounds as well. There was a playground along the west side of Cunningham Park, where we enjoyed running through the sprinkler. We also went to a playground in Whitestone, underneath the Whitestone Bridge. When visiting Aunt Evelyn and Uncle Meyer in Brooklyn there was a playground nearby with some moonscapes to climb on. P.S. 135 had its own playground with swings, a sprinkler, a sandbox, and monkey bars. We loved climbing on the monkey bars. I was lucky I was never hurt as the ground underneath was solid concrete! It was also in this park that Mark and I often played "scully," a game similar to shuffleboard, but with bottle caps.

SUMMER – 1960

From the 1920's through the 1970's the Catskill Mountains in upstate New York were known as the

Borscht Belt or the "Jewish Alps." With anti-Semitism still prevalent, many Jewish people felt scorned and ostracized, so they spent entire summers together at bungalow colonies in the Catskills and other upstate areas. The Altman family was no exception. Between 1960 and 1964 we spent four of those five summers at bungalow colonies, not in the Catskills but in upstate Westchester County and Dutchess County.

In the Summer of 1960 we went to a bungalow colony called Strawberry Mansion, located in Shrub Oak, Westchester County, near Mohegan Lake. Like all the other colonies it had an outdoor swimming pool, baseball field, a casino, wooded areas, hills, mountains, and other bungalows scattered over the area. We stayed in a 4-family bungalow. My dad worked Monday through Friday and usually came up only on weekends. He did have three weeks of vacation every August, at which time he stayed at the colony with us. My grandparents visited us often, sometimes driving up with my dad. Richie and I quickly made friends there. Next door there was a boy named Joey as well as a girl named Ellen ("Stupid Joey, stinking Ellen!" I used to exclaim). In the next bungalow there was a girl named Ronni, whom we nicknamed "Cry-Baby Ronni." Her parents were Joyce and Murray.

That summer was fun for me as I played with new friends, swimming, climbing rocks, collecting insects and lightning bugs, and other normal boyhood activities. My shyness and insecurity among strangers diminished, maybe because my mom and Richie were always nearby or because I was enjoying myself too much. With all the outdoor activities there was little need for television. The only TV was in the casino, where I used to go to watch reruns of the game show, "Video Village." The big hit record of that summer was "Itsy-Bitsy Teeny-Weenie Yellow Polka-Dot Bikini" by Brian Hyland. Ronni introduced me to the song, and we sang along whenever we heard it on the radio. Other hit records I recall at that time were "Volare" by Bobby Rydell and "It's Now or Never," by Elvis Presley.

Across the street and down the road from the colony was a miniature golf course next to a Carvel. We played that course a lot, and afterwards I would get a brown bonnet or cherry bonnet from Carvel. Those days of miniature golf and ice cream were my favorite days there. The closest city to us was Peekskill, where we often went grocery shopping. The summer of 1960 was a lot of fun, and I don't know why we never went back there.

FALL – 1960

That fall I entered first grade. There were five classes in each grade and the classes were ranked from five down to one, with class 1-5 having the smartest students and class 1-1 supposedly having the least smart. I was in class 1-1, not because I wasn't smart, but since I never talked in kindergarten the faculty members were unable to evaluate me properly. My teacher was Mrs. Eberle, an easy-going older woman.

Being a little older, I no longer needed my mom to take me to school. I either walked alone or with other kids I met along the way. There was one major street crossing, Francis Lewis Boulevard and Hillside Avenue. A very nice policeman named Frank would hold our hands and walk us across the street.

As I was now a full-time student I became more familiar with the school and its faculty. The Principal was Beatrice Lutz and the Vice-Principal was Mrs. Cloos. We often viewed them as old and stuffy, exclaiming, "Lutz the Klutz and Cloos the Goose is on the Loose!" The janitorial staff consisted of Mrs. Bopp and Mr. Bradsack, and Mr. Fanning was some kind of administrator. Mrs. Frolich was the reading teacher and Mrs. Glazer handled the audio-visual department.

Every morning the class began with the requisite "Good Morning Class," "Good Morning, Mrs. Eberle." We saluted the flag and recited the Pledge of Allegiance, usually followed by "My Country Tis of Thee" rather than the "Star-Spangled Banner." We then began our lessons, which this year included those Dick & Jane books ("See Dick Run. Run, Dick, Run"). Our class also included arts and crafts and finger-painting, and we always had a monitor in the room, a young lady who helped us get organized and escorted us in and out of classes. There was a "hot-lunch room" and a "cold-lunch room." The school provided lunches in the hot-lunch room, for which parents had to pay an additional fee. I never ate in the hot-lunch room as my mom always provided me with lunch to take to school and eat in the cold-lunch room. She would pack my metal lunchbox with a sandwich, a thermos of milk, and either a fruit or a piece of cake like a Twinkie. My sandwich was either salami, bologna, tuna fish, sardines, American cheese, or my favorite, peanut butter (creamy only…and no jelly!) A metal can of Scotch Ice was included to keep things cold. After lunch we played games in the lunchroom like "Simon Says" or "Go to the Head of the Class" before returning to our classrooms. In fifth or sixth grade there was a student in the lunchroom named Eleanor, who was loud, disheveled, nasty, and rude. I ignored her, and I got along fine with all the other students in the lunchroom.

The classroom layout was typical of 1960's New York City Public Schools with a blackboard in front of the class and an aluminum shelf underneath to hold the chalk and erasers. The American Flag stood next to the blackboard. On the side of the room were windows almost reaching the ceiling. As the top of the windows were beyond reach, a pole with a hook was used to open and close them. Opposite the windows were coat closets. In the back of the room we were assigned cubbyholes, where we put our hats, boots, scarves, gloves, lunch boxes, and other miscellaneous items. Our desks were made of wood, and as they pre-dated the age of ball-point pens there was a circular compartment in each one that years ago held inkwells for fountain pens.

Every day we went to physical education in the gymnasium, which mainly consisted of dodgeball and dancing. I did not care for either and especially hated the square-dancing. I particularly disliked those corny, childish dances we were forced to participate in, like dancing to "Skip to My Lou," "Did You Ever See a Lassie," and "The Paw-Paw Patch." For some reason that escapes me, Mrs. Eberle found it absolutely imperative that we learn how to skip and be proficient at it. I had difficulty in skipping as taught in the gym, so occasionally, while students were doing schoolwork or taking a test, Mrs. Eberle took my hand and walked me around the perimeter of the classroom, teaching me to skip. She would say "now let's step-hop...step-hop" as she skipped with me around the room. As my classmates looked over at me I felt awkward and embarrassed which didn't help me with my shyness and insecurity. I did indeed learn how to skip and, thank goodness, because my skipping prowess has been such an asset to me in later years!

On November 30, 1960, Randy Bruce Altman was born, giving me another brother. He was kind of a "roly-poly" baby and we enjoyed playing with him. My parents hired a nurse named June to come in everyday for the first few weeks to help take care of him. I remember watching my mom giving him his bottle, then burping him and putting him in his bassinette. I recall her diapering him with cloth diapers and safety pins. A local diaper service picked up the soiled diapers and left us clean ones. Hilltoppers nicknamed us "The Three R's," as in "Robbie, Richie, and Randy". Now, with my mom, dad, brothers, and my maternal grandparents nearby, our immediate family was complete. It would remain that way for the next six years.

Randy stayed in a crib at night with my parents in the large bedroom. Richie, having been out of a crib for quite a while, shared a double high-riser bed with me in the small bedroom. On school nights my parents made us go to bed at 8:00 pm, which we thought was a bit early. Richie and I talked in bed, sometimes for an hour or more, before saying goodnight to each other. I enjoyed lying awake in bed with him as we discussed school, friends, and TV shows.

WINTER – 1961

As I turned seven in 1961 I was still not done with wetting my bed. I often had to wake my dad up in the middle of the night so he could help me change my sheet. One day a representative from a company specializing in bed-wetting prevention came over to demonstrate a bed-pad and alarm system "guaranteed" to stop bed-wetting. One drop of moisture on the bed-pad triggered off an alarm. The bed-wetter would then wake up and go to the bathroom, then go back to sleep. I tried it for several days and it worked! My parents had made a very smart investment. Sometime later the bed-pad and alarm system were used by Richie, who shared the same problem. It worked for him as well.

At seven-years-old I was an avid TV viewer, watching mostly cartoons and other kiddie shows. One exception was early weekday mornings as I watched my mom exercising along with fitness guru Jack LaLanne on TV. My favorite program was Captain Kangaroo, a mainstay in my house every weekday morning. The show was on channel 2 at 8:00 am, and I watched it until I had to leave for school. The Captain had a "Treasure House," from where he would tell stories, greet farm animals, and indulge in silly stunts with the regulars on his show, including Mr. Green Jeans and the puppets Mr. Moose and Bunny Rabbit. Several cartoon shorts were featured, including "Tom Terrific" and "Lariat Sam." He also read from children's books, such as "The Story About Ping," "Curious George," "The Cat in the Hat," and "Mike Mulligan & the Steam Shovel," and had singalongs to various children's songs and current pop hits. I fondly remember his sing-a-longs accompanied by some crude visual animation: "Fuzzy-Wuzzy," "The Itsy-Bitsy Spider," "Alfred the Airsick Eagle," "The Green Grass Grew All Around," "Swinging on a Star," and "Big Rock Candy Mountain," just to name a few.

The number of cartoon shows I watched were so numerous that I couldn't mention them all, much less comment on them. My favorites included the Hanna-Barbera produced shows, "Huckleberry Hound," "QuickDraw McGraw," and "Yogi Bear." On Saturday mornings I watched cartoon shows such as "Crusader Rabbit," "Top Cat," and "Mighty Mouse." Other cartoons included "Little Audrey," "Little Lulu," "Felix the Cat," "Beany & Cecil," "Alvin & the Chipmunks," "Rocky & Bullwinkle," and "Casper the Friendly Ghost." I also enjoyed the exploits of the Loony-Toons gang (Bugs Bunny, Porky Pig, Daffy Duck, etc.)

Television at that time was filled with live-action Westerns. I eschewed this genre, maybe because of all the shootings and gunplay (I also thought "The Lone Ranger" was called "The Long Ranger.") However, I did enjoy some of the Saturday morning live-action adventure series, such as "Sky King," "My Friend Flicka," and "Fury." And let's not forget shows such as "Andy's Gang," "The Little Rascals," and "The Abbott & Costello Show."

An iconic cartoon show I especially enjoyed was "Popeye." I was not prone to violence, yet I enjoyed watching the brutality between Popeye and Bluto as they fought for Olive Oyl's affection. Since spinach gave Popeye his strength I asked my mom to buy me some, thinking it to be some dry leafy food item that I can shake out of a can just as Popeye does. Instead, she bought a wet, frozen, yucky-looking box of spinach, and I decided to pass on it.

My brothers and I had many toys and games, most of which were common among fellow baby-boomers. In our bedroom we had a wooden toy chest as well as metal shelving full of games. We had a slinky, which I played with in the hallway staircases. Before there were personal computers to do drawings and graphics there were Etch-A-Sketches, and we had a few of them. We had play-doh, silly-putty, Mr. Potato Head, and colorforms. We had Pick-up Sticks, Erector Sets, Lincoln Logs, and Tinker-Toys, which came in large cylindrical cardboard tins. The first board game I had was Candy Land. Games purchased later on included Chutes-and-Ladders, Parcheesi, Junior Scrabble, and Mousetrap, which was fun as we had to build a complex contraption on top of a board. We had yoyos, marbles, and spinning tops called Magna-tops, which we played with in the hallway. We also had a red robot-like toy made by Ideal called Mr. Machine, which was very popular for a while.

I loved music and I loved to sing, but only in the privacy and security of my home. I sang children's songs learned in school, like "Blinky the Traffic Light," "It's Raining, It's Pouring," and "Snowflake, Snowflake, Through my Window." I also enjoyed singing "This Old Man," "Ten Little Indians," "The Farmer in the Dell," "Sing a Song of Sixpence," and "I've Been Working on the Railroad," as well as more recently-penned children's songs, like "Found a Peanut" and "On Top of Spaghetti." My parents were music lovers and always encouraged us to sing.

SPRING – 1961

The spring of 1961 came as I continued with my schoolwork, TV watching, and playing with friends. My parents took us to a few more movies, including the original versions of "The Parent Trap," "The Absent-Minded Professor," and "101 Dalmatians."

Seven-year-olds are naturally curious, including explorations of their bodies and the bodies of others. One day I went into the bathroom of the B-Wing laundry room, along with Mark Levine, Stevie, Woody, and an unnamed younger girl who lived in our building. All of us but Stevie pulled down our pants, underpants, and panties as we exposed ourselves. Afterwards, we chased the girl into the Dover parking lot, trying to grab her pants and pull it down. While this may sound wrong and indecent, we were really young and it was just innocent fun.

As June arrived I graduated first grade showing very little improvement in my social behavior. I still hardly spoke in class, but at least I said "Robert" when asked my name, and threw in a couple of "yeses" and "nos." I still had a long way to go to overcome my depression, fears, and insecurity.

SUMMER – 1961

The summer had arrived and for some reason we did not go to a bungalow colony. Instead, I attended Hilltop Day Camp. I had a very difficult time there. Since I was born in January I was put in a group where the other campers were a year or two older than me. Mark Levine was in a younger group and I was disappointed I wasn't with him. Each morning all the groups congregated on Foothill Avenue in front of the Alpine. (Foothill Avenue was at the bottom of the hill; in later years that area was nicknamed "The Pits," as we used to hang out there and socialize.) We then took the camp bus to Cunningham Park, where we played softball, had cookouts, and went on hikes. My fellow campers included Johnny Spadaro, Michael Spielzinger, Marty Aber, Paul Fleiganspan, Gene Press, Ronnie Ortner, David Morganstern, Cliffy Zipin, and Eli Fishman. Eli, being my age, was the only camper who didn't pick on me. The others would hit me, call me names, and push me around. Marty Aber was the worst offender as he often knocked me to the ground and stuffed dirt in my mouth. Ironically, Marty and I became friends in later years.

By now I was starting to get over some of my shyness and depression, but I was replacing my anti-social behaviors with other inappropriate behaviors as I desperately begged for attention. I picked my nose, showing the results to the other campers. Johnny Spadaro, who was a real nasty kid, started calling me "Booga," a name that quickly spread throughout Hilltop and one I strongly disliked. I was glad when the summer was over.

FALL – 1961

In the fall I began second grade, class 2-3. My teacher was Mrs. Avery, another kind older woman. I was pleased upon hearing that Mark and I would be classmates.

There was a store in our strip-mall called Kirsans, which was basically our local 5-and-10-cent store. It was there where we bought our toys, water guns, arts-and-crafts materials, Elmer's glue, rubber balls, balloons, baseball cards, and all our school supplies. I purchased the required marble notebooks, pencil cases, erasers, and book covers for my textbooks. The book covers seemed pretentious as they always had the names and insignias of prominent universities on them. While most kids carried their books under their arms secured by a large rubber band, I opted to carry them in a briefcase.

I vividly remember the periodic fire drills and shelter drills, as well as something called a bomb drill, affectionately known as "duck-and-cover." The Cold-War was ongoing, Nikita Khrushchev headed the Soviet Union, the Cuban-Missile Crisis was about to begin, and the threat of nuclear war was on the minds of many Americans. With the bomb drill, as an alarm went off we ran under our desks and covered up our heads (I guess those wooden desks would really protect us from a nuclear blast.)

Whenever it was time to go into the hallway, whether it was for a drill, to the gym, or to assembly, the teacher would say, "Okay class, let's get into size places." The boys and the girls got into separate lines, with the shortest student in front and the tallest in back. I was about two-thirds of the way from the front. Mark, being slightly taller, usually stood directly behind me. Sometimes the boys and girls were required to hold hands while walking down the hallway, which most of us disliked. As the years went on, whenever we needed to cut into a line, we would say, "frontsy-backsy," thereby allowing us to maneuver our way in.

Some of my school activities included making potholders on metal frames, as well as making lanyards using long thin pieces of vinyl. I remember each morning the monitor passing out small containers of milk along with thin plastic straws, later collecting the empties. Also, every Tuesday was "bankbook" day, as the monitor distributed our personal bankbooks from Jamaica Savings Bank. We submitted about a dollar, then had the monitor collect the books. By the time I reached sixth grade I had a few hundred dollars saved, which I used to purchase a black-and-white Zenith TV set for my bedroom.

We were assigned special tasks on a rotating basis, like washing the blackboard or taking the blackboard erasers down to the basement where there was a vacuum "eraser-cleaning" machine. Sometimes we were assigned to the main office where we operated a special audio machine. This basically was a large radio, allowing stations to be broadcast and heard on speakers located in each classroom. When in operation it was usually set to station WNYE, the public educational radio station.

In addition to our hard-covered textbooks our learning was enhanced by stories, anecdotes, and puzzles found in the soft-covered "Think-and-Do" books and "Highlights" magazine. There was also the "Inkwell," the school's newspaper, as well as the "Weekly Reader," obviously published and distributed once-per-week.

In addition to Grand Union, Bohack, and Kirsans, we frequented many other stores in our strip mall. There were two banks, Manufacturers Hanover Trust and Ridgewood Savings Bank, a beauty parlor (where my mom got her hair done), a greeting card store, and an Italian Restaurant, Leonardo's. There was Joe's Barber Shop owned by Joe, a very jovial Italian gentleman, where we got haircuts for $1.25. Our haircuts were either crewcuts, semi-crew, or something called "butch." There was a bakery, fish market, dry cleaners, and our local pharmacy, later re-named Franhill Drugs. There was a German delicatessen called Utopia that later changed its name, first to Stanley's, then to Gene's. It was from there that I bought chocolate jelly-rings, candy dots, rock candy, and from the deli counter, as per my grandmother's directive, "American cheese, sliced very thin."

My favorite store was Goodies, a luncheonette which I affectionately called "the candy store." Goodies was a typical 1950's/1960's luncheonette: the back of the store had a Formica countertop with round stools that I would spin around. We ordered our hamburgers with French fries and maybe a cherry-coke. We had plenty of chocolate malts, ice cream sodas, and of course, chocolate egg creams. The front of Goodies had a candy counter with candies like Milky-Way, Chunky, and Good-N-Plenty for six cents. For a penny we got Bazooka bubble-gum. We enjoyed blowing bubbles while reading the little comics included with our gum. Opposite the candy counter was a newspaper/magazine rack along with some greeting cards and various knick-knacks.

Across the street from our strip mall were some other stores which I did not often frequent, or at least didn't until I was old enough to cross Hillside Avenue by myself. There was a furniture store, an optometrist, a bakery, a kosher deli, and a cute little shoe-repair store around the corner. There was also Sy-Ho Chinese Restaurant where we would dine in or order out. In 1961

Sy-Ho had a large fire affecting the whole block of stores. I remember looking out the window of my parent's bedroom, down 204th Street, and seeing the smoke rising from that block. Having recently seen an episode of "Lassie" about a quick-spreading forest fire, I was scared that the fire would spread to Hilltop. My fears increased as I anticipated flames appearing through the smoke. Fortunately, the fire was extinguished and Sy-Ho eventually re-opened.

Across Francis Lewis Boulevard was Jay's Diner, our local diner and hang-out. It was very well-known among New York City residents. Whenever we went upstate or out of town and told people we had an apartment near Jay's Diner, they knew exactly where we lived.

As 1961 was coming to an end, I went to three more movies: "Flower-Drum Song," "Snow White & the Three Stooges," and around Christmas time, the remake of "Babes in Toyland." My dad also took me to my first Broadway show, "Young Abe Lincoln," which we saw with my dad's co-worker, Aaron Roses, and his young daughter.

WINTER & SPRING – 1962

In 1962, as I was turning eight, television was as important to me as ever. Several live kid's shows were on the air after school. As I arrived home around 3:15pm, the iconic "Soupy Sales Show" aired, followed by "The Sandy Becker Show." I loved Sandy Becker, as he adopted a wide range of alter-egos like Norton Nork, Hambone, and The Professor. He appeared in short skits and mocked current pop hits like "Mr. Bass Man" and "Leader of the Pack." Included in his program was a live-action short, "Diver Dan," an underwater adventure. His show also included some memorable commercials, including one for Bonomo Turkish Taffy, and one for Beechnut Gum featuring the Four Seasons singing "Let's Hang On."

My late-afternoon TV viewings also included Dick Tracy cartoons. I had a hand-puppet of Joe Jitsu, one of the characters on the show. Following Dick Tracy was "The Three Stooges," hosted by "Officer" Joe Bolton. My friends and I loved the Stooges, and of course Curly was our favorite. At 5:30pm, channel 11 aired "The Adventures of Superman" starring George Reeves. Superman was my favorite superhero, and I watched every episode over and over through the years to the point I knew almost all the lines. My late-afternoon TV viewing ended at 6:00pm; that's when the TV news came on, my dad came home from work, and my mom began serving dinner.

My usual weekday breakfast consisted of milk and cold cereal, usually Sugar Smacks, Sugar Pops, Cocoa Krispies, or Sugar Crisp (Kellogg's and Post Cereal were sure big on sugar!) I would sit at the dining room table, watching Captain Kangaroo and reading the back of the cereal boxes. When I got a little older I ate breakfast while reading excerpts from the Golden Book Encyclopedia. Sometimes I collected cereal box tops, and when I gathered a certain amount I submitted them for various prizes. For lunch on weekends I sometimes had "fruits & cream" instead of a sandwich. My mom would buy a box of Birdseye frozen fruit, then mix it with sour cream. While I used to love fruits & cream, Richie preferred a similar meal, "bananas & cream."

My grandmother was an excellent cook and a great baker. I remember her apple cake with soft, flaky crust. She also made these delicious soft lemon cookies. She taught my mom how to cook and bake, but my mom was never as good as she was. Dinner, or supper, was basically meat, potatoes, and a vegetable like peas and carrots, with soda to wash everything down. I especially enjoyed having pasta for dinner, such as elbow macaroni or wagon wheels. I did not like some food items like liver, ham, or the vegetables, but I had to eat them, not only for nutritional reasons, but because "there are starving children in the world." I was pleased after cleaning my plate, knowing that all the children in the world will no longer go to bed hungry! About an hour after dinner we had "milk and cake," maybe a cupcake, a Ring Ding, or a slice of apple pie. Milk was plain whole milk, but I always liked it better with a little Cocoa-Marsh or Bosco added. My mom also made chocolate pudding, Jello, and served us Junket, a custard-like dessert. I always enjoyed licking the spoon after my mom made the chocolate pudding.

Orange drink, or Orangeade, was very popular in the 1960's. One such orange drink came in small white cardboard containers with metal rims. I always enjoyed drinking from those containers, especially on hot summer days. We also drank lots of milk. Quart containers of milk were purchased for 25 cents from a vending machine in our basement. We also had bottles of whole milk, skim milk, chocolate milk, and seltzer delivered to our front door. We ate all types of bread, but especially Wonder Bread because, like the commercial said, "It builds strong bodies in eight ways."

Since my mom didn't drive, most of the food shopping was done at Grand Union, Bohack, or Gilbert's, as they were all in walking distance (Gilbert's was a few blocks away near our public library). With my dad we were able to drive to other supermarkets such as Daitch/Shopwell in Fresh Meadows and Hills on Francis Lewis Boulevard near the Blue Bay Diner. I called Hills "the store with the rainbow" due to its arch-shaped façade. For dairy products we often went to Gouz in Elmont, where they had a small farm with some animals in back. We got farm-fresh eggs, milk, cheese, and bread. Their slogan was, "Gouz, Rhymes with Cows." Of course we never left a supermarket without my mom collecting some S&H Green Stamps, which she saved in a booklet until they were ready for redemption.

We went clothes-shopping at Mays and Macy's in Jamaica. I liked going to Macy's because we got to park on the roof of the store. We also shopped at Masters in Lake Success, Great Eastern Mills in Elmont, and Korvette's in Carle Place. I loved going to Korvette's because my parents would buy each of us a Charlotte Rouse from a food vendor outside the front entrance. Charlotte Rouses were round sponge cakes topped with whipped cream and a cherry. You first ate the whipped cream and cherry, then pushed the cake up through a round cardboard to eat the rest.

About once-per-year we went shopping at Fortunoff, located in Brownsville, Brooklyn, under the "el" train. Fortunoff sold a mixture of housewares, hardware, and other merchandise, and while my parents shopped there Richie and I played around, inventing silly phrases like "where's the powder, in the hose." Nearby Fortunoff were several outdoor push-cart vendors selling the most delicious knishes ever. We made sure to have them with added salt and mustard.

We went to various clothing stores and shoe stores, shopping for our parents as well as for us. My shoes were either from Buster Brown or Tom McCann, and my sneakers were either Keds or PF Flyers. My brothers and I were rambunctious and detested clothes-shopping and trying on shoes. We often ran around the stores playing hide-and-seek, although we tried our best to behave for fear of getting spanked. After an hour or two of shopping I became restless, tired, and fidgety. I couldn't wait to leave the stores and go back home to the comfort of my home and my TV.

Back in the relative privacy and comfort of the car and my home, I resumed my singing. While my parents always supported my singing, I was also encouraged to play a musical instrument. My dad took me to a small music studio in a residential area of Jamaica where he enrolled me in music lessons. The studio gave both guitar and accordion lessons and I opted for the guitar. My dad bought me a dark-wood Fender guitar with nylon strings. I had one-on-one instruction as I learned to play songs like "Glow Worm," "Beautiful Dreamer," "Tennessee Waltz," and "Rock Around the Clock." Despite my dad's insistence I didn't practice at home as much as I should have. After a few weeks I discontinued the lessons, but I did continue playing around on my guitar for several more years.

Music may have still been on my mind as my parents took us to see the filmed version of "The Music Man" starring Robert Preston. We all loved the movie and thought Preston's performance and charisma was what made the movie so appealing.

Also in 1962 we took a boat trip on the Circle-Line around Manhattan. I enjoyed travelling under all the bridges, and seeing the Statue of Liberty, Empire State Building, and Yankee Stadium from the Hudson and East Rivers. My dad especially enjoyed seeing Columbia University and Grant's Tomb, as he would repeatedly recite the bad rhetorical joke, "Who is buried in Grant's Tomb?" Home movies show me enjoying the experience. I'm also shown with my front teeth missing, as Dr. Grossman recently extracted them.

SUMMER – 1962

As the summer arrived I was pleased to hear we'd be going to another bungalow colony as I did not want another year at Hilltop Day Camp. We spent the summer at Sunny House, another colony near Shrub Oak. Like Strawberry Mansion it had an outdoor pool, ballfields, casino, and a lot of wooded areas. I made two friends there, Eddie and Bart. Eddie built a tent behind his bungalow and I spent some overnights in there with him. Eddie, Bart, and I spent a lot of time hiking and exploring the woods, then coming home very dirty. There was a teenager there named Mark, who was very nice and taught me how to play "Heart and Soul" on the piano in the casino. Many dogs were on the property, including a German Shepherd named Gilbert, a beagle named Jack, and Tippy, a small black dog. Gilbert once bit me on the hand as I was petting him. The wound was superficial, but as I got scared my mom took me to a doctor for some antiseptic. I stayed away from Gilbert the rest of the summer.

For the last few years our family car was a light-blue Chevrolet. One day, as my dad was coming up for the weekend, he surprised us by driving up in a brand new car, a gold 1962 Chevrolet Belair, which replaced our old car. This would remain our family car until it was stolen seven years later.

While up at Sunny House we went on a day trip to Mount Beacon. We parked at the bottom, then took a special tram up to the top of the mountain. Once at the top we had lunch and enjoyed a spectacular view as I recall us being higher than some of the clouds!

I enjoyed the summer a lot. I sang a lot of songs, many of which my parents taught me, like "Carolina in the Morning," and "I'm Gonna Sit Right Down and Write Myself a Letter." I went swimming, played a little ball, and flew a kite. By the end of August I was back in Hilltop and ready to start third grade.

FALL – 1962

As I graduated second grade I was showing some improvement in my social behavior. I wasn't raising my hand in class, but at least I was talking with classmates and speaking in complete sentences. As the faculty recognized this, I was moved up in rank: third grade, class 3-4. I was pleased that Mark would be in my class for the second consecutive year. My teacher was Mrs. Lugar, a refreshingly younger woman.

All Jewish boys from Hilltop began Hebrew School the same year they started third grade. Hebrew School lasted for five years, with students having their Bar-Mitzvah sometime during their fifth year. The classes were held from 4pm to 6pm at the Holliswood Jewish Center, a Conservative synagogue located on Francis Lewis Boulevard, two blocks up from Hilltop. My first-year teacher was Miss Bernstein, a stern-looking young woman with horn-rimmed glasses. We nicknamed her "B.O. Bernstein" as she had body-odor. Miss Bernstein called us all by our Hebrew names. My Hebrew name was always written in Hebrew letters, but in English it's Chaim Reuven.

That first year we learned the Hebrew alphabet, discussed the history of Israel, learned about the Jewish holidays, and read stories from the Old Testament, from Abraham to Noah's Ark to Moses and the Ten Commandments. Our classes always ended with the singing of Hebrew songs, either "Ein Keloheinu" or the slow or fast version of "Adon Olam."

I was not a very religious person. My mom and her parents grew up in a religious environment, but not so my dad. Both my parents believed in G-d, but my dad instilled in me that it's more important to be kind and have good morals and character than to just follow all

51

the Jewish traditions. I had some ambivalence about the existence of a Supreme Being. Nevertheless, I had no issues attending Hebrew School other than the teacher's unpleasant odor. Also, I knew most of my classmates, and Mark Levine was in my class as well. Besides Mark, my classmates included my friend Marvin Berk, Mitchell Feldman, Eli Fishman, Gary Fishman, Mark Hauser, Jeffrey Benson, Kenneth Erlich, Andrew Zeger, and Wayne Eisen, a short blond-haired guy who always called me "Alti-Baby."

Every Saturday morning Junior Congregation was held at the synagogue, or "shul," followed by the Adult Service. We were all encouraged to attend the junior service, and I did attend it on a semi-regular basis for the next few years.

When I wasn't attending services I was home watching Saturday morning TV. Besides the cartoons I watched "Just for Fun," a two-and-a-half hour show hosted by Sonny Fox. The show was inspired by camp "color wars" as two teams of kids in blue and gold jumpsuits competed in various stunts and contests. There were two shows airing Sunday mornings that I watched religiously: "Let's Have Fun" aired on channel 11 and was hosted by Chuck McCann. The show opened and closed with the host singing "Put on a Happy Face." He did skits and imitated various comic-strip characters like Little Orphan Annie. I especially enjoyed the inclusion of "Flash Gordon," the movie serials from the 1930's and 1940's. My favorite weekend show was "Wonderama," airing on Sunday mornings on channel

5. Sonny Fox hosted that show as well. The four-hour program had a little bit of everything: spelling bees, Simon-Says, limbo contests, tongue-twisters, mad-libs, art instruction, guest celebrities, and magic demonstrations from "The Amazing Randi." As I didn't have a remote control I continually had to get up to change channels from channel 5 to channel 11 and back. It was worth the effort to check out these wonderful children's programs.

I also have to mention "Shari Lewis & Friends," airing mostly on Saturdays. Shari Lewis was a wonderfully gifted ventriloquist and puppeteer, and I enjoyed her "friends," Lamb Chop, Charlie Horse, and Hush Puppy. There was a common thread present in all these live-action children shows. Besides entertaining us, Soupy Sales, Bob Keeshan (Captain Kangaroo,) Sandy Becker, Sonny Fox, Shari Lewis, etc. would talk to us about morals and values, respecting parents and other grownups, saying please and thank you, learning the Golden Rule, and saying our prayers before bed. They were done in a way that was neither preachy nor condescending, and I respected that.

As 1962 was coming to close I saw the movie "The Longest Day" with my dad, and "The Wonderful World of the Brothers Grimm" with both my parents. I also went to see the animated "Gay Purree" and the re-release of "Pinocchio."

WINTER – 1963

As I was turning nine-years-old, my leisure activities did expand beyond TV and movies. My dad bought us a Lionel train set which we set up in the living room. It was fun assembling the tracks and running the freight cars around. We also had Aurora slot cars, tiny electric racing cars with motors which ran on a plastic racing track. A plug-in transformer was attached to provide power. My brothers and I had fun racing the cars around our living room track. My friend Marvin Berk had a racing set as well, and we used to race his cars in his apartment.

My dad and I did some projects together. We went to Kirsans, where we bought model airplanes as well as a Gemini-model space capsule. We spent many evenings together assembling them at the dining room table. It usually took several evenings to complete each project. My dad was also into collecting vintage stamps. Every month or so he received stamps in the mail, and I helped him catalogue them and put them into little clear envelopes. They then went into a large loose-leaf binder. My dad also spent some evenings teaching me chess. He would checkmate me all the time. Those evenings with my dad were very enjoyable and gratifying.

My mom was not without her own leisure activities as she played mah-jongg regularly with other mothers in the building. They played in different apartments on a rotating basis. When playing at our house my mom always chased me back into my room when I came out to watch them.

My parents occasionally took a well-earned break from work and child-care as they went out, alone or with other couples. Mrs. Sussman, a middle-aged woman who lived in our building, babysat us. I didn't like her coming over because she always kissed me. And, unlike my Aunt Hattie, there was no monetary payoff for sacrificing my cheeks to her kisses.

As I continued third grade I remember the yearly "open school week" when the moms visited the classrooms during a lesson. I was always nervous seeing my mom walking in and sitting in the back of the room. I had to remember to look alert and attentive, and of course, not suck my thumb. I remember Mrs. Lugar introducing us to cursive writing during that day of open-school week. One day Mrs. Lugar mentioned what was perceived as a slight speech impediment; I had trouble pronouncing the "L" sound, substituting it with a "Y" sound, as in "yeave me ayone." She sent me to speech class, taught by a Mrs. Bernstein (no relation to B.O. Bernstein). Mrs. Bernstein tried to teach the class to pronounce the "L" sound by having us recite "La la la la la sang Lila. Lovely lilies lined the lane." I did not like speech class and only went the one time; my speech impediment eventually subsided by itself. I also recall Mrs. Luger taking the class on a trip to the Ridgewood

Savings Bank on Main Street in Flushing. We met with a bank representative who taught us the basics of banking and finance.

My unhealthy desire for attention resulted in a worsening of inappropriate behavior, like pulling girls hair or fidgeting and making noises in class. Not knowing how to handle this, Mrs. Lugar consulted with the faculty as well as my parents. The results of their discussions was to refer me to an outside professional for further evaluation. Once-per-week I was excused from class as I took the Q76 and Q44 buses by myself to Queens College in Flushing. There I met with a psychologist, who gave me the usual psychological tests like the Rorschach Test, word-associations, and showing me ink blots, asking me what I see. These weekly visits continued for a few months, after which the recommendation was that I discontinue my visits and instead see a private psychotherapist (of course at my parent's expense). Suffice it to say, these weekly visits at Queens College did nothing to help me, and only resulted in my missing some classwork. I would eventually see a private psychotherapist, but for now the solution to my bad behavior had to lie elsewhere.

SPRING – 1963

In May of 1963 we had our yearly visit to Dr. Irwin Harris, our family doctor and pediatrician. I hated that one day every May as we drove down to Far Rockaway, where a lawn jockey in front of the Doctor's house greeted us. I'd sit in Dr. Harris's waiting room, nervously looking up at the Norman Rockwell paintings and hoping that I don't get a "needle." Most of the time I did indeed get an injection, whether it be for polio, a booster shot, or a tetanus shot. I always cried as my parents held me down. As we left the office Mrs. Harris gave us lollipops, but that did little to ease the trauma. As was common back then, Dr. Harris made house calls. When we were sick, whether it was the German measles, the Grippe, or some other illness, he'd come over with his black bag in hand. As I said, although I did experience all the common childhood diseases, I was fortunate to be a physically healthy child.

My parents were raised in an era where physical punishment was common. My dad's father often beat him for misbehaving. He had a slight scar on his forehead from a time when his father hit him. Unfortunately, I was also a victim of this mentality as I was physically harmed by my parents and maternal grandfather (but not my grandmother). My dad punished us by spanking or slapping us in the face, sometimes in public. When my brothers and I misbehaved my dad or my grandfather took off their strap and hit us. My mom hit us too, with a belt or just her open hand. There's one particular instance I remember well: because of my fears and low self-esteem, I had difficulty speaking someone

57

else's name aloud. I felt it was presumptuous as I wasn't worthy enough to speak the name of someone who was better than me. There was a new kid in class, Dale Nussdorf. I told my mom about the new boy, and when she asked me his name I refused to answer. She took out a belt and started hitting me, shouting "Tell me his name! Tell me his name!" I cried and cried and refused to answer. My grandmother came in the room and tried to stop her, but my mom pushed her away and kept hitting me. Finally, I screamed out "Dale! Dale!" and the hitting stopped.

My parent's favorite numbers appeared to be 1, 2, and 3. When disciplining us, they'd say something like, "If by the time I count to three, if you're not...you're getting a spanking! One...Two...Three!" True to their word, if we didn't do as we were told by the time they reached three, we were indeed hit or spanked.

Looking back, I try not to hold any resentment towards my parents and grandfather. They were raised in an era where physical punishment and discipline was the norm, and they did the best as they knew how. They tried to love us, teach us, and care for us to the best of their ability and, all things considered, they did a good job.

On a lighter note, my parents spent part of the spring of 1963 taking us to see four new movies: "How the West Was Won," "Son of Flubber," "A Boy 10-Feet Tall," and one of my all-time favorites, "Bye Bye Birdie." I loved the music from the film and especially enjoyed seeing Dick Van Dyke, Ann-Margret, and Bobby Rydell starring in it. Right after Ann-Margret opens the film by singing the title song, there are outdoor scenes of Queens and Manhattan which to me really captured the look and feel of that era.

May of 1963 arrived and, as in every spring, the yellow petals of the forsythias in front of the Dover were turning green, meaning summer was not far away. In June I completed third grade and kept my hope up that we'd be going upstate again for the summer. I was pleased to hear that we'd again be spending the summer at a bungalow colony, this one being a little further north, in Dutchess County.

SUMMER – 1963

View Hill was located in Hopewell Junction, near Sylvan Lake. It was one of several colonies located at or near the lake, including Pleasant View, Holiday, Somerset, Spiros, Forest Lake, and Dutchess Acres. We were in bungalow #5, a small 3-bedroom bungalow located near the middle of the property. My parents slept in one bedroom, my brothers shared another, and I had the smallest bedroom to myself. North of our bungalow was a playground, an arts and crafts building, and other bungalows. Looking out my bedroom window to the south I could see the casino, as well as a long path going down the hill, past the ball fields to the large outdoor swimming pool.

Unlike the previous colonies, there was a children's camp, appropriately named View Hill Day Camp. The camp director was Milton Pincus, who originated from Brooklyn and was up there with his wife and three kids, Charles, Lori, and Cindy. My counselor's name was Ethan, a tall, twenty-something, very likeable man. Each weekday morning I woke up to the sound of "Reveille" coming from the front-office loudspeaker. This was followed by Mr. Pincus exclaiming over the loudspeaker, "Everybody up up up up up! It's a beautiful day at View Hill Day Camp!" He followed that by announcing some of the day's scheduled activities. I ate my breakfast (usually cold cereal), then my brothers and I congregated around the flagpole, along with the other campers. Campers took turns raising the flag, which was followed by the Pledge of Allegiance. Our morning activities included hiking, arts and crafts, archery, tetherball, handball, and contests like tug-of-war, three-legged races, and scavenger hunts. We returned to our bungalows for lunch, until another announcement came on the loudspeaker: "All campers down to the flagpole!" The afternoons activities included softball and swimming, and we returned to the flagpole at the end of the day as the flag was lowered.

On the first day of camp we learned the camp song:

"We welcome you to View Hill Camp

60

We're mighty glad you're here

We'll send the air reverberating

With a mighty cheer

We'll sing you in, we'll sing you out

Till you will raise a mighty shout

Hail! Hail! The gang's all here

And we welcome you to View Hill Camp."

Some of us wise guys changed some of the lyrics to, "We'll kick you in, we'll kick you out, and stuff your mouth with sauerkraut. Hail, hail, the garbage pail." Mr. Pincus also taught us an Indian chant, which went, "Ungee Dibonga, Hig Dig-a-dig-a-dig, Heffle de-peffle Deffle, Ee-ow!" (I'm guessing Mr. Pincus made this chant up).

Camp was a lot of fun as I made some new friends. The ones I remember most were the Lilianthals', brothers Gary, Jay, and Brian, who was Richie's friend. Gary was distinctive in that he had one brown eye and one blue eye. I remember winning the annual scavenger hunt. My prize was a giant Sugar-Daddy candy. I wanted it all for myself, but my mom cut it up so I could share it with the other campers.

Folk music was very popular in the early sixties, especially in camp settings. We sang songs made famous by Woody Guthrie, Pete Seeger, Bob Dylan, and others, such as "This Land is Your Land," "Michael, Row the Boat Ashore," "Blowing in the Wind," and "He's Got the Whole World in His Hands." Being an all Jewish camp, we learned many children's songs inspired by the Bible and the Old Testament: "Rise and Shine (and Give G-d Your Glory Glory,)" "There Were Three Jolly Fisherman," "Who Did Swallow Jonah," and "Joshua Fought the Battle of Jericho." Mr. Pincus also presided over the children's Hebrew services in the casino, where he taught us Hebrew songs like "Shalom Chaverim," and "Zum Gali Gali."

In 1962, Peter, Paul, and Mary came out with their first record, a self-titled album. My parents bought the album, as did many fellow View Hill families. By 1963 it became the most popular album in our colony. Whether in camp, in the bungalow, or in the car, we sang "If I Had a Hammer," "Lemon Tree," "500 Miles," "Where Have All the Flowers Gone," "The Cruel War," and others. We found meaning and inspiration in many of these songs, which included a lot of anti-war themes.

As in previous years, my dad came up only on weekends except for some vacation time in August. My grandparents often came up with him and were somehow able to find room in our bungalow to sleep. One day Richie's best friend Mitchell Seiler, who lived in the Cumberland with his parents and younger brother Gary, came up to visit for a weekend, probably coming up with my dad on a Friday night and going back home with him on Sunday.

Every Friday night at 7pm the staff put up a big screen inside the casino, where they showed cartoons for the young kids, like Bugs Bunny, Woody Woodpecker, and Road Runner. Afterwards the kids left for bed and then it was time to show movies for adults. My parents let me stay as they felt I was old enough to watch the adult movies. The films were usually light romantic comedies starring Doris Day, Marilyn Monroe, Rock Hudson, Cary Grant, and Jack Lemmon, although they sometimes showed a more dramatic movie like "To Kill a Mockingbird." It was nice being able to stay up later than usual as I felt more grown up.

Weekends upstate often included running family errands. Sometimes we drove about twenty minutes to Poughkeepsie to go shopping. While we rarely ate out, there was a small Italian restaurant near View Hill called Joanne's, which had great pizza. Most evenings my dad, as well as other fathers, barbequed on those old charcoal grills. I watched the smoke rise up high as he applied the lighter fluid. We had hamburgers, hot-dogs, lamb chops, and steak. Sometimes we toasted marshmallows. My mom usually spent the evenings playing cards, mah-jongg, or canasta with the other mothers as we played with our friends. On many Sunday mornings I walked with my grandfather across the street to Spiros, the only local bungalow colony with a news stand. As my grandfather bought a newspaper, he also bought me a lollipop, chewing gum, or some other candy. My grandfather and I often took quiet walks together around the area, which bring back very pleasant memories.

On July 20th a total solar eclipse occurred over the northeastern United States. We were all excited about viewing the eclipse and were disappointed to find out that eye damage can occur upon viewing the eclipse directly. We all scurried around collecting shoe boxes and putting holes in them, thereby allowing us to view an image of the eclipse in safety. As this became a joint venture with the neighbors, it became a fun event.

One other fond memory I have is of Dugan's, a bakery truck that visited all the bungalow colonies, selling various baked goods. I remember one warm sunny morning when the truck pulled up. My mom bought a box of vanilla cupcakes with different icings. I looked over the cupcakes, trying to decide which one to eat first: the one with the chocolate icing, the vanilla icing, or the strawberry icing. I always ate the icing first. It's amazing that such seemingly insignificant moments from so long ago can bring back such warm and vivid memories.

As the summer wound down and we began packing up our things, I said goodbye to my new friends and fellow campers, hoping to see them again next summer. I was very happy to hear that we would indeed be returning to View Hill next year! I had spent the whole summer away from my Hilltop friends, in a bungalow with no TV and no air-conditioning, yet it was my best summer to date. Best of all my depression and insecurities were at a minimum for most of the time.

FALL – 1963

The fall of 1963 arrived as I began fourth grade, class 4-4. I was back to having an older teacher, Mrs. Calvert, and I was glad to be in the same class with Mark for the third consecutive year. The class set-up was a little different. Instead of having three rows of desks, they faced each other, allowing for more interaction with fellow classmates. I also began my second year of Hebrew School. My new teacher was Mr. Diskind, a tall, lanky, older man with a big nose.

Richie was starting kindergarten this year, which I think had expanded to full days. I took Richie back and forth from school, saving my mom the task of taking him. Our walks to and from school were pleasant, except for one particular day as we were walking home from school. Bruce Arnold, who was a year older than me and lived in the Alpine, started hitting Richie. Rather than defend my brother I just stood there frightened. Bruce eventually stopped the hitting, but I felt guilty for not defending Richie by fighting back against Bruce.

My shyness and passiveness was like catnip for the older neighborhood bullies. One day an older kid, Ralph Herman, had his big dog chase me down Foothill Avenue, scaring the heck out of me. Another time Harry

Mindlin and Gary Fishman, who were usually nice, forced me to pull down my pants and urinate in the parking garage of the Everest Building. My fellow ex-campers from Hilltop Day Camp often pushed me, hit me, and called me names as they encountered me in the street. One day I saw Johnny Spadaro hanging out in front of the Fairmont with some friends. Johnny exclaimed, "It's too bad Altman isn't black. We could call him Black-Booga."

One day after telling my dad that Michael Spielzinger had been picking on me, he came out, ran down the hill, and confronted him. After that Michael never picked on me again. (Kudos to my dad! I only wished he confronted some of the other bullies as well).

As I've said, my parents were big music lovers, and they especially loved Frank Sinatra. When my mom was a teenager she was known as a "bobby soxer," as she lined up with other zealous girls to see Sinatra perform at the Paramount in Manhattan. My father had a lot of albums from the Big Band era, including ones by Bing Crosby, Glenn Miller, and Benny Goodman, and had several albums of Broadway musicals as well. He also had many albums by conductor and musician Mitch Miller, who had a TV show on Friday nights called "Sing Along with Mitch." I used to sit on the living-room carpet as my dad sang along to his records. I didn't care much for the records but to appease my dad I listened anyway. My dad's favorites included, "There is a Tavern in the Town," "Be Kind to Your Web-Footed Friends," "Beer-Barrel Polka," "Goodnight Irene," and "When

the Red Red Robin Goes Bob-Bob-Bobin' Along."
These songs were kind of corny and outdated, but my
dad loved them anyway.

Besides Mitch Miller, there were many other records
we enjoyed listening to. Allan Sherman was a Jewish
comedy writer and television producer who became
famous for releasing several albums which parodied
other songs. His big hit single was "Hello Muddah, Hello
Faddah," released in 1963. All his records were infused
with Jewish humor. We bought his first two albums, "My
Son the Folk Singer," and "My Son the Celebrity." Mark
and Sammy's parents also had his albums, and we
listened to them in each other's apartments. My favorite
selections included "Sarah Jackman," "Harvey &
Sheila," "My Zelda," and "Al & Yetta." Growing up
listening to Jewish humor and Jewish comedians, our
parents enjoyed his records even more than we did.

When I think about hanging out in my old living
room and listening to records, I'm reminded of the
apartment furnishings. The wall-to-wall, olive-green,
living-room carpeting was part of the décor that can best
be described as mid-20th-century traditional. Besides the
large TV console, with a wall-to-wall mirror over it, our
living room had a couch with a fold-out bed. At each
end were two large mahogany-wood tables with old-
fashioned lamps and lampshades. In front of the couch
was a dark wooden coffee table. The opposite wall had
a wall unit with a stereo phonograph as its centerpiece.
At the ends of the wall unit were two red-upholstered

armchairs with carved dark wooden legs. As was common at the time, the couch and chairs were often covered with clear plastic for protection. As recliners were not yet popular, my dad had a soft, dark-green easy chair, along with a light-green hassock. It was in this chair that he watched TV, read the newspaper, and had father-and-son discussions with us. To brighten up the room the walls were painted beige, but by today's standards I think the living room would be described as rather drab.

The kitchen was brighter, with white walls, silver appliances, and a yellow step-stool. The dining room was wall-papered, and a light blue wall was present in both the large bedroom and the small alcove leading into it, an area we called the "dressing room." The door frame of my bedroom featured a chinning bar, frequently utilized by my brothers and I to improve our upper-body strength.

We did not have any air-conditioning until the mid-sixties, when one was installed in the living room window. My parents placed fans in strategic positions around the apartment in hopes that some of the cool air from the air-conditioner would be deflected into the bedrooms. That idea never worked very well, and I had to make do with a small oscillating fan to cool my bedroom on those hot summer days and nights.

Around this time I attended a couple of Bar-Mitzvah receptions of some cousins of mine whose last names I believe was Gelt. I was pretty bored as I sat on the children's dais, watching the adults doing the Hora, followed by some corny group dances that were popular at wedding receptions, the Alley Cat and the Bunny Hop. Some adults tried teaching me the "cha-cha." I was not really interested in dancing, although I did enjoy watching teenagers on TV doing "The Twist," and other current dance crazes on American Bandstand.

MOVIES

Around this time my dad took me to see the first two theatrically released James Bond films, which were playing as a double feature, "Dr. No," and "From Russia With Love." With the action, car chases, explosions, gadgets, and the charisma of Sean Connery, what wasn't to like? I loved both movies and became a big 007 fan. Whenever I attended a Bond movie, I fantasized being a secret agent. I went into the theater lobby and pretended to be spying on people, as I'd sneak around the pillars and stairways.

I went to several war movies and dramatic films alone with my dad. We often sat in the back of the theater as he explained the parts of the films I had difficulty understanding. I always enjoyed the special bond with him as the two of us went out together.

Around this time my dad took me to see the re-release of "20,000 Leagues Under the Sea," and I went with my brothers and friends to see "The Three Stooges Go Around the World in a Daze," as well as the new Jerry Lewis movie, "Who's Minding the Store?" Most of the movies I saw were either in Jamaica, Queens Village, or Fresh Meadows. Jamaica had the Valencia, a large, opulent, old-fashioned theater, as well as the smaller Alden theater. Queens Village had the Community and Queens theaters, while Fresh Meadows had the Meadows theater.

Jerry Lewis was my favorite comedian at the time. I eagerly watched his films whenever they aired on television: "The Delicate Delinquent," "The Geisha Boy," "Don't Give Up the Ship," "The Errand Boy," and of course, "The Nutty Professor." I didn't like his films with Dean Martin as much, probably because they were in black-and-white.

Sometime around 1963 as I was walking into my building through the basement entrance, a twenty-something man came up to me. He asked me if I would help him deliver newspapers. I was frightened and shook my head no, but he kept insisting I come with him. Being naïve and gullible as I was I went with him, first onto the elevator, then onto the staircase. Once on the staircase he put his hands on my shoulders and started doing knee bends, telling me he needed me to help him exercise. At that point I got scared and ran up the stairs to my apartment and told my mom what happened. She called the police, and a few minutes later a cop showed up at

70

our door. I told him what happened and gave him a description of the man. He told me I had been molested and he would file a report. I think the fact that I didn't see any newspapers should have tipped me off that this guy was unsavory. I felt lucky nothing more serious happened, but I was still shaken up a little bit.

This molesting incidence was a little frightening and had a negative impact on my naïve innocent years. Around this same time a major national tragedy occurred, further affecting my naivete. November 22nd was a typical school day. I was sitting in class when an announcement came over the speaker that President Kennedy had been shot, and we were being dismissed early. We all left the building in shock (on my way home some jerks started hitting me, telling me I killed the President). Once home my family and I watched TV intensely as Walter Cronkite announced the tragic news: that President John F. Kennedy was assassinated in Dallas, Texas while riding in a presidential motorcade, and Texas Governor John Connally was seriously wounded. We watched over the next 48 hours, as Lee Harvey Oswald was charged with his murder, later to be fatally shot himself by Jack Ruby. I went up to Marvin's apartment to watch some of the funeral but watched most of it with my family. The assassination evoked stunned reactions, both in this country and worldwide. My parents and I were big fans of the Kennedys, and words cannot describe how shocked and saddened we were as was the rest of the nation. Vice President Lyndon Johnson was sworn in as President, and the nation struggled to recover from this tragedy as best it could. A few days after the Kennedy assassination and funeral, my normal activities of schoolwork, friends, and TV resumed.

Despite the fun I had upstate and with friends, the times I felt the most safe and secure, if not the happiest, would be the days I stayed home sick from school. Some mornings I woke up feeling a little feverish or congested, but not bad enough to be physically suffering. I would whine to my mom, "Mommy, I don't feel good!" She took my temperature (rectally) and I crossed my fingers that I wouldn't have a high fever, but just enough for her to let me stay home. When she allowed me to stay I felt content and happy as I can now spend the day being with my mom and watching TV. If I had fever she gave me St. Joseph's Aspirin for Children, which she mixed with a little orange juice. If I had a sore throat I had Luden's wild cherry cough drops which tasted like candy. I then settled down on the living room floor to watch TV for most of the day.

During the early 1960's the weekday morning TV schedule stayed pretty consistent. At 9:00am channel 2 had "Dennis the Menace," followed by one of my favorites, the now classic "Leave it to Beaver." I loved Beaver and Wally and got a kick out of Eddie Haskell. At 10:00am I watched either "I Love Lucy" or "The Lucy Show," usually followed by "The Donna Reed Show." Following that would be various game shows, and at noontime, "Jeopardy" and "Let's Make a Deal." My TV viewing would then reach a lull as my mom

72

watched soap operas, her favorite being "As the World Turns." I hung out with my mom, watching her cook and clean, until my regular shows returned after 3:00pm. I was truly a "mama's boy," and felt safe and secure being home with her rather than in the outside world (after all, I could spend a whole day without bullies or teachers with dirty looks). To this day, I still watch reruns of those old situation comedies I grew up with and I still get a kick out of them. Reflecting back on those more innocent times I get that "warm fuzzy feeling" as I think of my childhood and being home with my mom.

It may appear paradoxical in that I felt so safe and secure with my mom when there were those occasions of being physically punished by her. My mom did give me lots of hugs and kisses, and her unconditional love and caring for me far outweighed the negatives.

WINTER – 1964

The year 1964 began as I went to see two movies: the animated "The Sword and the Stone" and the comedy classic, "It's a Mad Mad Mad Mad World," seen in Manhattan in wide-screen Cinerama. My brothers and I laughed hysterically near the end of the picture as most of the cast dangled from the top of a fire truck ladder.

My Sunday evenings were very predictable. Every other week or so my dad brought in food from Sy-Ho Chinese Restaurant. We always ordered chicken chow-mein and my dad ordered peppered steak. We also had egg drop soup, won-ton soup, spare ribs, egg foo young, fried rice, almond cookies, and fortune cookies. On TV we watched "Lassie" at 7:00pm and "My Favorite Martian" at 7:30. Simultaneously, channel 7 aired "Walt Disney's Wonderful World of Color." At 8:00pm channel 2 aired the long-running variety show, "The Ed Sullivan Show," which featured just about every famous person on the planet. After that show ended at 9:00pm, I took a shower, then went off to bed.

I don't specifically recall the evening of February 9, 1964, but I'm sure I was watching Ed Sullivan as usual. Of course that was the night Sullivan introduced John, Paul, George, and Ringo to American audiences. The Beatles opened their segment with "All My Lovin'," and with records like "I Want to Hold Your Hand," "She Loves You," and "Can't Buy Me Love," heard all over the radio, American teenagers were soon hooked on Beatlemania. The current pop-music scene was about to change, as several British rock & roll bands invaded America. Suddenly, records frequently played on the radio by Frankie Avalon, Chubby Checker, Connie Francis, and the Drifters were replaced by songs from the Dave Clark Five, Gerry & the Pacemakers, Herman's Hermits, and Petula Clark. Although I wasn't a Beatles fanatic at the time (at least not yet), I heard their records all the time and really enjoyed them. I was very upset when my friends went to see the movie, "A Hard Day's Night" without asking me along. I never found out why they didn't invite me, although a year later I went with them to see the Beatles' next movie, "Help!"

My grandparents made a move, as they left their dingy first floor apartment on 164th Street, moving into a nicer third floor apartment on 169th Street, also in Jamaica. It was much brighter and safer, and my grandfather was still in walking distance to the subway. They remained in this apartment for the next ten years, after which they moved to Florida.

My grandmother and I spent many nice moments together. She took me to several movies, we went shopping together at Macy's or Lamston's, and when the weather was nice we took walks in Goose Pond Park, located near Jamaica High School. Every year around Christmas she took me to Gertz department store on Jamaica Avenue. Inside the store was an area called "Enchanted Village," where a little toy train took us around to see Santa's workshop, Christmas displays, and animated elves and reindeer. My grandmother was always generous in buying me ice cream, sucking candies, and other treats. I always enjoyed my outings with her.

SPRING – 1964

Spring had arrived as I continued with my classwork. Because the desks in fourth grade were arranged differently, I sat face-to-face with Mitchell Feldman. Mitchell, whom I called "Feldman," lived in the Ivy Ridge, had reddish hair, and was in my Hebrew School class. We quickly became good friends. By now I was starting to eat lunch out, rather than "brown-bagging" it every day. Starting in the spring Feldman and I often ate lunch together at the kosher deli on Hillside Avenue. I always ordered hot-dogs and French fries. The fries were not spicy, but they were always very hot. Today, whenever I eat very hot fries I think back to that deli. Unlike myself, Feldman was a good athlete, and after lunch I watched him play handball in the school playground until it was time to return to class.

Being an active and adventurous boy, I had my share of bumps and bruises. I was not a klutz, but with my feet sticking out a little I wasn't the most graceful person on two feet. Once I was playing in the Dover playground with my friend Eddie Wolkis when I fell off the see-saw, resulting in a large gash over my left eye. As blood was dripping down my face Eddie escorted me to the doctor in the Cumberland, where I was treated. Another time I was climbing a barbed-wire fence behind the Ivy Ridge, as I wanted to explore a water tower there. As Eli's brother Teddy looked on, the top of the fence went into my armpit. I rushed myself to the doctor, who closed up the wound by putting in three stiches. I fell off my bicycle a couple of times, and had many cuts, scraped knees, and bruises. The common antiseptics used at that time were iodine, which stung like heck, and mercurochrome, which left an ugly red stain. I usually opted for Bactine, which was safer, painless, colorless, and nearly as effective.

On April 22, 1964 the "1964/1965 New York World's Fair" opened at Flushing Meadows Park on the same site as the 1939 fair. The fair's theme was "Peace Through Understanding," and was noted as a showcase of mid-20th century American culture and technology. It featured 140 pavilions as well as numerous water fountains, rides, and restaurants. We went about three or four times in 1964, and a few times the following year.

I was very excited the night before going for the first time. My dad bought a map of the fair, and we looked over his shoulder with great anticipation as he planned where he would park and what attractions to visit. The next morning we parked near the lake, then walked to the Florida Pavilion where we saw a live porpoise show. We then crossed over the bridge to the General Motors Pavilion where we took a ride called "Futurama," travelling into the future. The Ford Pavilion provided us with a ride through prehistoric times, and we rode on the US Royal Ferris wheel. Other pavilions included IBM (where we went into a giant "egg"), Johnson's Wax, Traveler's Insurance (the big red umbrella), General

Electric, Bell Telephone, and the Kodak Pavilion where we walked on a moonscape. At the Pepsi-Cola Pavilion we saw "It's a Small World," the now-iconic attraction of Disneyland and Disney World. We went on the Log-Flume ride, and at night watched the fireworks at the Pool of Industry.

We went to the RCA Pavilion where a picture of my dad was taken randomly, thereby entering him in a contest. He ultimately won second prize, a new stereo record player. Since we had a record player they gave him a new tape recorder instead. While there we also ran into Mark, the teenager who taught me how to play "Heart and Soul" on the piano at Sunny House.

In many ways the World's Fair was very commercialized, with companies advertising their products and services. Still, as I drive past that area today and see the Unisphere and New York State Pavilion still standing, I'm reminded of the joy and excitement I had during those visits.

My schoolwork continued, and in June I graduated fourth grade. I was very disappointed when told that my fifth- grade class would be 5-3, taught by Mr. Paxson. Not only would I be ranked one class lower, but both Mark Levine and Mitchell Feldman would be in a different and higher-ranked class, 5-4, taught by Mrs. Goldrich. I was upset that my two friends would not be in the same class as me, and I had no choice but to accept it.

SUMMER -1964

July 1964 began as 21,000 troops were sent into South Vietnam, essentially marking the beginning of the Vietnam War. Also, President Johnson signed the Civil Rights Act of 1964 into law, abolishing racial segregation in the United States. As for me and my family we'd be going back upstate to View Hill Bungalow Colony for the second and last time.

Most of the kids I knew from last year were back, including the Lilianthal brothers. Milton Pincus was back as camp director, but sadly my counselor from last year, Ethan, did not return. I had another nice summer as the day camp continued with sing-a-longs, athletic activities, swimming, and various competitions. We also spent one overnight in the woods, sleeping in sleeping bags. As I was a poor athlete and did not enjoy sports, Mr. Pincus tried very hard to make an athlete out of me, spending extra time with me doing batting practice at the ballfield. The Friday night movies continued and, as I was a little older, I attended the Saturday Bingo nights with the adults. I also started hanging around the soda machine by the main office as I began an extensive bottle-cap collection with another friend of mine.

One of my fellow campers was named Bob Freed. Once he met Richie, Bob started calling him "toad nose," due to Richie's pug nose. He would sing, "Everybody calls him toad nose" over and over. Richie became really upset by his constant teasing, as well he should have. I became a traitor to my own brother as I would also occasionally call him toad nose over the next several years. Being upset by kids calling me Booga, I should have been more empathetic towards Richie, and to this day I regret teasing him like I did.

The only other negative memories are my yearly summer encounters of insect bites and of poison ivy, poison oak, and poison sumac. We always kept bottles of Calamine lotion handy. I usually healed quickly, but there was one time I had a serious case on my knees, resulting in my parents taking me to a local doctor for treatment.

It amazes me that certain sounds, sights, and smells bring back memories of those summers in the country. When I smell something musty, I'm reminded of opening the bungalow at the beginning of summer. The smell of grass reminds me of lying in fields, looking for four-leaf clovers, watching insects crawl through the grass, or picking little green apples from the apple trees. A skunk's foul odor brings back memories of past summer encounters with that smell. Even the smell of rubber reminds me of the rafts and inner-tubes I used in the swimming pool.

Our bungalow colonies did not have the same reputation and legacy as the more famous and opulent ones in the Catskills. The Concord, the Raleigh, Grossingers, and Kutchers had big-name entertainment, gift shops, valet parking, and restaurants. At the same time, there were many similarities between them and us: the day camps, the athletics, the games, the movies, the swimming, the Jewish services, the bar-be-ques, and the ubiquitous mah-jongg and canasta games played by the moms. I remember my time in the bungalow colonies with great fondness. I also feel a little melancholy as their popularity has all but disappeared with the changing times.

FALL – 1964

In September I began fifth grade. Concurrently, I started my third year of Hebrew School with Mr. Marvin Lazar, who was also the director of the school. My fifth-grade teacher was Mr. Paxson, a bald, 52-year-old, who curiously was the only male teacher in the school. Mr. Paxson pretended to be tough when in reality he was very fair and kind. He always threatened to hit us with a ruler or throw an eraser at us, but of course he never did. He taught us a lot about history, as well as World and U.S. Geography. Whenever the class was stumped by a geography question, he either called upon Eli Fishman, Michael Stern, or myself as we usually knew the answer. As all male students throughout the school were required to wear ties, whenever we came to class without one, Mr. Paxson had a closet full of loud, showy, wide ties which he made us put on. Mr. Paxson was my favorite elementary school teacher.

By now my bouts of depression had diminished somewhat, and fortunately some of my bad behaviors were also lessening. I now spoke well, without any speech impediments and in complete sentences, both with teachers and classmates. I also had an easier time making new friends. Despite this noticeable improvement some depression issues still remained, and there were still some moments of inappropriate behavior as I continued seeking attention. My parents took the advice of previous faculty consultations and sent me to a private psychotherapist.

His name was Dr. Kalin, a middle-aged, heavy-set man who had a first floor office located off of Queens Boulevard in Forest Hills. My parents took me there every Saturday morning. In order to avoid any teasing or embarrassment I kept my visits a secret from my friends. Some mornings as we were leaving our building, Mark or Marvin would be outside, and they'd say something like, "Hey Robbie! You want to play some stickball?" I would tell them I had to run errands with my parents, but I still felt ashamed and embarrassed knowing where I was going. I knew if Mark ever found out he'd laugh at me and tell all our friends I was seeing a psychiatrist.

Dr. Kalin played checkers and other games with me, and we had some long discussions. My visits with him caused me to feel shame and embarrassment and I felt like I was a misfit. My mom and dad never fully explained to me what the goals and benefits would be in seeing him, only that I had to see him. I wished they had sat me down and told me what was to be gained by these visits, while at the same time assuring me that I was a normal young man.

After about a year he and my parents decided there was nothing further he could do for me. My sessions with Dr. Kalin did very little to improve my behavior and emotional state. It did seem to improve Dr. Kalin's financial status, as after several sessions he moved into a nicer office!

HOLIDAYS

As with every American child, holidays were important. Elementary schools emphasized the significance, as well as the fun, of holidays. Lincoln's Birthday and Washington's Birthday were discussed in school every year, which usually included a song called "Little Month of February." On Valentine's Day the girls in the class were "encouraged" to hand out greeting cards to each boy, and vice-versa. My dad celebrated every Valentine's Day by purchasing a big heart of assorted chocolates for my mom, usually bought at Franhill Drugs. At Easter time we painted eggs in class and sang songs like "Here Comes Peter Cottontail" and "Easter Parade." My dad sometimes bought a large chocolate Easter Bunny for us to share.

The Passover holiday was of course discussed in much detail in Hebrew School. Our family usually had one Seder each year, either at my grandparents or at home. One year Mr. Lazar invited us to his apartment for a Seder with his family. It was convenient as he lived in our building with his wife Celia and his son Adam, who was Randy's age. As expected, Mr. Lazar's Seder was more involved and more orthodox. I also enjoyed Passover as my mom made us "matzo brei," the Jewish dish made with fried matzah and eggs.

As candy lovers, Halloween was a favorite holiday of my brothers and me. We usually all went trick-or-treating together, covering both the Dover A-Wing and B-Wing. I often dressed as a cat or tiger, with a plastic mask held around my head by a rubber band which was always breaking. Back then there was little concern about eating unwrapped candy, and we especially loved those little candy corns. Upon returning home we would dump the contents of our trick-or-treat bags on the dining room table. My parents would help divvy them out, and by the end of the evening a lot of it was eaten. By the following day most or all of the candy was consumed. Once I turned twelve or thirteen, instead of getting candy it was

84

"Trick-or-Treat for UNICEF!" Whatever coinage I received I would promptly send to that charity.

On Election Day Hilltoppers voted in booths set up in the Dover social room. It became kind of a social event as a spread of bagels, cream cheese, salads, and chopped liver were set up on a nearby table.

Thanksgivings were usually spent at my grandparent's apartment. My grandmother was a great cook, so the food was always delicious and plentiful. As he did at Easter, my dad bought us a large chocolate turkey. I also liked Thanksgiving because I got two days off from school!

Every year during Hanukkah menorahs could be seen in many windows of Hilltop, with most of them utilizing orange bulbs. We were told in Hebrew School that we should only have menorahs with real candles, and that's what my family had. We lit the menorah and displayed it on top of the refrigerator for the required eight days. As Hilltop was almost entirely Jewish, very few windows had Christmas lights or decorations. Regardless, the management got into the holiday spirit as the front facades of each building were decorated with red, green, and gold Christmas lights. Even though we didn't celebrate Christmas my family and I still enjoyed the holiday, whether it be singing holiday songs or watching Christmas-themed TV programs. Each holiday season my dad took us out at night, driving around nearby neighborhoods to look at the Christmas lights. It was exciting to see all the lights and Christmas trees, especially a large tree in Jamaica Estates, as well as one in Cunningham Heights. I added holiday songs to my home repertoire, singing "Jingle Bells," "Silver Bells," "Santa Claus is Coming to Town," and "Rudolph the Red-Nosed Reindeer." I understood that Christmas was a Christian holiday celebrating the birth of Christ, and I obviously wasn't into the holiday's religious meaning. Regardless, I did enjoy the songs and festivities.

During three or four of the holiday seasons, my parents took us to Rockefeller Center to see the giant Christmas tree. We drove to the subway station in Queens, then took the train to 57th Street in Manhattan. With great anticipation and eagerness my brothers and I ran over to the tree. We gazed at it with our mouths open, in awe of its size and brightness. We watched the ice skaters skate around the rink near the tree, and we looked at the Christmas displays in the department store windows. We were so excited and joyous that we became oblivious to the cold and the crowds. One special visit was in December of 1964 when, prior to visiting the tree, we went to the premiere of the film "Mary Poppins" at Radio City Music Hall. It immediately became my favorite Disney movie. I loved seeing Julie Andrews and Dick Van Dyke starring in it, and I loved the music as well.

I saw several other theatrical movies in 1964, including the Disney films "The Three Lives of Thomasina" and "Emil & the Detectives." Other films included "Father Goose," "Fate is the Hunter," the science-fiction film, "First Men in the Moon," and the re-release of the classic "The Bridge on the River Kwai." My dad had the soundtrack album to "The Bridge on the River Kwai," and we listened to it at home as he whistled along to "The Colonel Bogey March."

WINTER – 1965

With the Winter of 1965 upon us, my dad did what he usually did on snow-covered Sunday mornings: he took us sledding. The three of us lined up on our wooden Flexible Flyer: Randy in front, Richie in the middle, and me in back. My dad pulled the sled down the hill and over to Goodies, where he bought several newspapers, including The New York Times, Journal American, Herald Tribune, and Long Island Press. He then pulled us back up the hill to the Dover. As we got bigger it must have gotten increasingly harder for him to pull us up the hill, but he was obviously strong enough and able to manage.

Living on a hill provided an ideal environment for sledding. On snow-covered days 204th Street would be filled with kids on all types of sleds. We built forts and snowmen and had numerous snowball fights. Prior to going out our parents always made sure we were dressed properly. My mom put plastic bags over our shoes so our boots would slip on more easily. Once we had on our boots, coats, hats, scarves, and gloves, it was playtime! While the adults were busy shoveling out their cars or putting chains on their tires, we were having a ball. On snow-covered days, for the kids of Hilltop it was truly a winter wonderland.

There's one particular evening that I look back on with special fondness. One cold, clear winter evening my mom answered the doorbell. It was Mark Levine. He had a round, silver, saucer sled under his arm, and he asked me to go sledding with him. We went to the Dover playground which was covered with a sheet of ice. We took turns sledding down the ice and had a great time. Afterwards we said goodnight and said we'd see each other in class the next day. A specific, simple evening of fun with a good friend can bring back such warm memories, even fifty-or-so years later.

TELEVISION

The 1964-1965 TV season included some of my favorite programs. My Monday night viewings included "The Andy Griffith Show" and "The Lucy Show." Tuesday nights included "Mr. Novak," "The Red Skelton Show," and "The Man from U.N.C.L.E." I wrote a fan letter to David McCallum, who portrayed Illya Kuryakin on the show. A few weeks later I received a "Man from U.N.C.L.E." coloring book, as well as a membership card and photographs of David McCallum and Robert Vaughn, who portrayed Napoleon Solo on the show.

Wednesday night viewings included what became my all-time favorite program, "The Dick Van Dyke Show." This classic comedy show, created by Carl Reiner, still holds up today with its intelligent humor, first-class scripting, and a terrific cast, including Rose Marie, Morey Amsterdam, and Mary Tyler Moore.

Thursday nights included "The Flintstones," "The Donna Reed Show," "My Three Sons," "Dr. Kildare," and "Bewitched." Friday nights had "The Addams Family" and "Gomer Pyle, USMC." Saturday nights I watched "Gilligan's Island" and "The Jackie Gleason Show." By this time "The Jackie Gleason Show" was airing live from Miami Beach, and was alternately called, "Jackie Gleason's American Scene Magazine." The show featured many zany characters such as Crazy Guggenheim, as portrayed by Frank Fontaine. Also included were musical "Honeymooner" segments, featuring Gleason, Sheila MacRae, Art Carney, and Jane Kean. I enjoyed many other TV programs during that era, too many to mention. I truly feel that the 1960's were the Golden Age of television.

By the mid-sixties most scripted TV programs were being filmed in Hollywood, rather than New York City. However, many game shows, talk shows, variety shows, and news programs were still being taped in New York.

I went into Manhattan with Mark and Eddie, along with their moms, to see live tapings of two shows. We saw a taping of the game show "I've Got a Secret," hosted by Garry Moore, at CBS Studio 59. On another occasion we went to a taping of "The Garry Moore Show," a variety program starring Garry Moore and "Candid Camera's" co-host, Durward Kirby. That show was taped at the Brooks Atkinson Theater on 47th Street. The shows were exciting to watch, although the view of the stage was partially obstructed by the many cameras being utilized. I also recall going to NBC studios at Rockefeller Center to get tickets for some other game shows. I don't remember if I saw any additional tapings.

Since TV was so important to me, I experienced mild panic attacks on those occasions when it was on the fritz. Back then TV sets were run by cathode-ray tubes, rather than solid-state. We were able to test the tubes ourselves, as my dad and I brought them to Franhill Drugs where they had a vacuum tube-testing machine. You found the bad tube and bought a new one, then put all the tubes back into their proper sockets. When we were unable to fix the TV ourselves, we called upon our local TV repairman, George Lind from Cunningham TV. George would come over with his tools and mirrors and was usually able to get the set working again quickly.

Sometimes on Fridays and Saturdays I stayed up late watching TV. I couldn't watch past 1:00am as all programming ended at that hour. After the final program of the night, all stations played "The Star-

Spangled Banner," followed by a test-pattern. The test-pattern remained on the screen until the following morning when regularly scheduled programming recommenced.

Obviously I was very passionate about television, spending several hours-per-day viewing my favorite shows. That being said, l also enjoyed reading, as I joined the Weekly Reader Book Club. Every month a book arrived in the mail. Some of the titles included "Assignment: Spy," "True Life Adventures," "Henry and the Clubhouse," "Homer" (a book about a boy who loved doughnuts, not the ancient Greek author), and a series of books about a family called "The Happy Hollisters." I also read some of "The Hardy Boys" books, as well as a book based on TV's "Leave it to Beaver." A couple of years later I began collecting a series of soft-covered books called "How & Why Wonder Books." These books mainly dealt with science, and included titles like "Rocks & Minerals," "Dinosaurs," "Weather," "Stars," and "Mammals."

One book I especially enjoyed was a yellow hard-covered book, titled "Kids Say the Darndest Things" by Art Linkletter. The book was based on the author's interviews with children on his TV show. Charles Schulz's drawings of Charlie Brown and the "Peanuts" gang provided the book's illustrations.

Reading books and encyclopedias about other parts of the world led to my strong desire to travel and see other lands. I had a large hard-covered Rand McNally

World Atlas, along with a globe. I periodically turned to different pages in the atlas and imagined myself visiting that part of the world, whether it was South America, Africa, Australia, or some other state in the nation. Not recalling much of my first trip there, I had a strong desire to go back to California. I kept pestering my dad about travelling there, maybe staying with Max and Bess again. My dad told me I'd have to wait, as his parents were not in the best of health (even though they had recently travelled to Europe!) It wasn't until 1973 when I was nineteen that I finally got to go back to California, travelling there by myself.

SPRING – 1965

Eddie Wolkis was probably the smartest and most mature out of all my friends. We called him "Mr. Ed," a reference to the TV show about a talking horse. We later nicknamed him "Canary" because of his hair color. My friends and I spent of lot of time hanging out in Eddie's bedroom, which he shared with his brother, Stevie. Mark, Eli, Sammy, Woody, and I were regular visitors. Eddie played the viola in Junior High School, but prior to that he was an accomplished guitar player. We used to enjoy hearing him play songs like The Ventures' "Walk Don't Run." As Eli was the best vocalist in our group, Eddie taught him to sing the lyrics to the Beatles' song,

"This Boy," while he accompanied him on guitar. A lot of the early Beatle records remind me of those times hanging out in Eddie and Stevie's bedroom.

Eddie and Stevie had a pet garter snake named Hermana, which they kept for several years. They also had a small metal safe on their dresser, which I once marked up with a magic marker in another stupid, immature attempt at getting attention. They also had puzzles and games to play with, including a cool electric football game. We occasionally hung out in Mark's bedroom as well, where he had several games, including "Password," "Operation," and a TV trivia game.

We decided to form a club, electing Eddie as President and Mark as Vice-President. I was the treasurer, as I collected 15 cents every week from the members. Joanne Solomon was appointed secretary, but she moved away soon after the club started. Sammy, Stevie, and Woody were other semi-regular members. We had weekly meetings where we discussed what games to buy, what movies to see, and what outings to go on. We met in our bedrooms on a rotating basis. Our moms always brought out bowls of pretzels, potato chips, or cheese doodles for us to snack on. Our club was nameless, but I informally called us "The Dover Boys."

As I said previously, although Marvin Berk was one of my best friends, he was also a troublemaker. His real father either died or left when he was an infant, and his mother, Renee, re-married a man named Sam Wurtzel. His stepdad spoiled him by buying him lots of toys and electrical equipment. Marvin used to brag that his stepdad was some type of doctor, when he was actually an elevator mechanic. Sam eventually left Renee but continued a close relationship with Marvin. Marvin had one sibling, an older sister Linda, who unlike Marvin was smart and had her act together. Marvin was the neighborhood kid who threw eggs at doors during Halloween, threw snowballs through open windows, and once threw pretzel nuggets at our super (he had a great arm with all that throwing!) On the 4th of July he lit firecrackers and cherry bombs, then threw them under women's skirts as they walked by. He loved to fart in people's faces, and he was also able to turn his eyelids inside out, which was really gross. He also liked to urinate on the staircase and in the bicycle room.

Mark, Eddie, and others from the Dover disapproved of Marvin's behavior and excluded him from our club. Marvin, feeling ostracized by his fellow Dover boys, sought out friends from other buildings, like Robert Blair, the son of the Cumberland's super, as well as Mark Lebowitz and Ricky Weinberg. My friends, feeling that Marvin was a bad influence on me, decided to hold a "trial" to determine if I should continue to be friends with him. We gave him a "subpoena," ordering him to appear at our next club meeting, held in Mark's bedroom. Club members gave "testimonies" and Marvin, the defendant, pleaded his case. The final verdict was that Marvin was indeed a bad influence, and I should no longer be friends with him. As Marvin ran out of the apartment in tears, I was told I had to choose a "blood brother" and I chose Eddie. We went down to Eddie's apartment to officially become blood brothers. Unable to stick our fingers, we just rubbed our fingers together under running water, prompting Eddie's mother Bernice to say, "Okay, now you're water brothers!" Marvin, feeling scorned and angry, tried forming a rival club with kids from other buildings, but that effort was short-lived. Suffice it to say, a few months later I was friends with Marvin again, our club dissolved, and life in Hilltop went on. It's nice now to look back at all the fun, as well as the silly trials and tribulations we all went through.

I spent a lot of the first half of 1965 in theaters, seeing no less than eight movies. My dad took my friends and I to see the World War II movie "The Train" starring Burt Lancaster. He took me to see "36 Hours," starring James Garner, a film about the D-Day Invasion. I also saw the films "Those Calloways," "The Satan Bug," "Dear Brigitte," "Crack in the World," and "In Harm's Way," which I saw with my mom. My dad and I went to Manhattan to see the premiere of "Goldfinger," one of the classic James Bond movies.

My father was the most popular dad among my friends, as he took them and I on several outings. While my mom stayed at home with my brothers, he took us to the Hayden Planetarium, to museums, and to several movies, with all expenses paid by him. He and my friends were very informal, as they called him "Sonny," the same name my mom and grandparents called him.

He left my Hilltop friends with great memories of him, with his kindness and generosity.

I went on numerous outings with my parents and my brothers. Besides Kiddy City we went to other amusement parks, including several visits to Rockaway's Playland and to Coney Island. I remember Coney Island's Steeplechase Park, where we waited on a line for an hour or more before going around a track on their electric horses. I went on Coney Island's iconic roller coaster, the Cyclone, which was a little scary. Of course we ate hot-dogs and those famous French fries at Nathan's Famous. We once went to Idlewild (now Kennedy) Airport to watch the planes take off and land. We went to beaches many times, especially Jones Beach. The waves were always a little scary, but building sandcastles was fun. As we were leaving to go home my parents would wrap a towel around us while we took off our bathing suits and put on a pair of shorts. Sometimes I'd hang out naked in the back seat until we were halfway home!

The Bronx Zoo, Hayden Planetarium, the American Museum of Natural History, The Statue of Liberty, the top of the Empire State Building, the Met Cloisters in Manhattan, the top of the RCA building, and the Central Park Zoo were some of our other outings. We also attended a few New York Yankee games at the old Yankee Stadium, as well as some New York Met games, then played at Shea Stadium. Richie was especially fond of trains. He always got excited when, during our outings, we passed by a moving passenger train or freight train.

Being three rambunctious boys packed into the back seat of a Chevy, there was bound to be some horseplay. My dad warned us, "if you boys don't behave you're gonna get a licking!" If we continued to misbehave he pulled the car over, turned around, and proceeded to hit us. My mom usually said nothing as she had issues of her own. She was not a good passenger and often complained of headaches and dizziness while riding in the car.

While in Manhattan we often ate at the Horn & Hardart's Automat. The Automat was a dining staple in the 1960's, with its marble countertops and floors, as well as steel and glass vending machine grids displaying sandwiches and desserts. The milk and coffee came out of fancy golden spouts. I liked putting the nickels into the coin slot, then having a cheese sandwich or a piece of cake come out for me.

We had Chinese food at either Sy-Ho or King-Yum Chinese Restaurant on Union Turnpike. For Italian food we went to Salvatore's on Hillside Avenue, across the street from our strip mall. Salvatore's was small and intimate, and I especially loved their pizza and their spaghetti with meat sauce.

One of my favorite eateries was Happy Robin, located on Hillside Avenue and 217th Street, in Queens

Village. Happy Robin was a family-style restaurant with both indoor and outdoor seating. Inside was a buffet line and a brick-oven grill, cooking up great burgers and steaks. They also served great cheesecake. I remember my brothers and I excitingly opening the umbrellas on the outside tables as my parents went inside to order our food. Sadly, Happy Robin went out of business in the early '80's.

FRIENDSHIPS & JEALOUSY

In 1965 my jealousy and immaturity became front and center. As I said, in fourth grade I became good friends with Mitchell Feldman. In addition to our one-to-one friendship, he included me in his group of friends from the Ivy Ridge: Joel Goldstein, Ted Harris, Stuart Levy, Robert Murmelstein, and others. As Feldman was no longer in my class, our friendship dissolved. Furthermore, he became good friends with Mark Levine. I soon became intensely jealous of their friendship. If I had handled it in a mature way, I wouldn't have let it bother me. Rather I would have searched out other friends, old and new. However, my jealousy and immaturity took over my brain. I proceeded to spend many days after school "spying" on Feldman. I hid behind bushes or behind a building watching him as he played ball or hung out with his buddies. When someone caught me spying I told them I was writing a book about him. Later on I actually started writing a book. I bought a little notepad, and headlined the first page with, "Objective: to stop Feldman from being friends with Mark Levine." I proceeded taking down notes: the day, time, and location of a Feldman spotting. One day Feldman cornered me in front of my building and took away my notepad.

In retrospect, I wish I hadn't wasted those days spying on him, but rather had spent my time more productively, like playing with friends who wanted to be with me. There was a little "James Bond/Secret Agent Man" in me, so there was some thrill in my espionage. In any event, about a year or two later, Feldman moved with his family to Bayside. I only saw him one time after that, at an evening indoor-swimming trip with a Jewish Youth Group, also attended by Mark.

Although Mark Levine and I were good friends, his popularity and his many friendships were a source of constant jealousy for me. While all my friends were confined to Hilltop, Mark had several other friends from school who lived outside of Hilltop, including Richard Rand, Fred Stansfield, and Neil Shacht. He also had a close friend Raymond, whose parents were friends with his, a cousin Michael, and a close cousin named Fay. There was even a little girl from across the street, Robin Palmer, who had a crush on him. Mark would often subtly let me know that he had more friends than I did, causing further friction between us.

As June arrived I completed fifth grade. I was told that my sixth-grade class would be 6-3, whereas Mark would be in class 6-4. Although there were some issues between Mark and myself, I was still sorry we would not be classmates.

SUMMER – 1965

My parents decided that we were finished spending our summers at upstate bungalow colonies. I assume they felt that, as we were older, we'd be better suited going to a local day camp or sleepaway camp. Richie and Randy began attending Cross-Island Day Camp, with most activities being held at Cunningham Park. I was told I would be attending Wel-Met sleepaway camp, located in upstate Narrowsburg. They decided I'd go for just the three-week session in August rather than the full six-week session, maybe to make the adjustment easier for me. Although I really didn't want to go, I didn't make a fuss about it. Besides, Mark would be away for the summer at Camp Lakota, and there wouldn't be many kids at home to play with.

On July 1st, my grandmother took me to see the film "Genghis Khan" (an odd choice for a movie to see with one's grandmother). The next day I went with her to Manhattan to see the movie "My Fair Lady" (a better choice, since a grandmother would usually take a kid to a musical rather than a war picture). Other films seen around this time included "The Great Race," "Those Magnificent Men in their Flying Machines," the new Jerry Lewis film, "The Family Jewels," and the World War II movie, "Von Ryan's Express," seen with my dad. The rest of July was spent playing ball with friends, running errands, and making several trips to the beach. I also spent a few nice days with my family back at the World's Fair, now in its second and final year.

The day came for me to leave for sleepaway camp. Wel-Met, which had divisions in Narrowsburg, Barryville, and Silver Lake in Sullivan County, was basically a low-cost camp for Jewish boys and girls. Unlike other more luxurious and specialty camps, it was more rustic and down-to-earth. My parents drove me up to camp, where we were introduced to some of the administrators. As soon as they kissed me goodbye and left, I had an immediate sense of fear and loneliness. As I had never been away from my parents for more than a few hours, I felt alone and frightened.

I was in bunk #52 with about ten other kids. The only names I recall was a kid named Morey and a kid whose last name was Shapiro. My counselor was Steve Newman, a tall twenty-something man who wore yellow sneakers. Other counselors included Stan Bach, Mike Press, Bernie Alter, and a Native-American named Grover. The boy's bunks were in a separate area from the girls; I heard rumors of panty raids going on among

101

the older kids, which I was much too young to think about.

We went hiking, had an overnight in the woods, played softball, participated in color-wars, and went swimming in the adjacent lake. There were handball courts, an infirmary, a cafeteria, and a clubhouse, where the kids and staff once performed some numbers from "West Side Story." There were two songs frequently sung at camp: "I'm Henry the VIII, I Am," the current hit record by Herman's Hermits, and the folk song, "Greenback Dollar," made famous by The Kingston Trio. Grover especially liked singing "Greenback Dollar" as he'd make up his own words.

Despite what appears to be a lot of fun activities, I continued being scared and lonely. My usual low-grade depression escalated, and I became increasingly shy and withdrawn. The bathrooms and showers were in a separate building, and I was the only kid to shower with a bathing suit on. My bunkmates seemed to enjoy exposing themselves and comparing their penises. My shyness prevented me from participating, resulting in disapproval and scorn from the others. One day I overheard them plotting to grab me and pull my pants down. I told my counselor what they were planning, and he later made them leave the bunk as I changed my clothes. This resulted in even more resentment towards me and made the rest of my time there very uncomfortable.

The fact that I was not a good athlete and didn't much care to participate in any scheduled sports made it even more unbearable. I remember one day during softball feeling very sad, depressed, and homesick. I fell to the ground and started crying. Steve Newman came over to console me. Among other things, he told me that if I became more interested in playing sports, as well as watching and understanding professional baseball, football, and basketball, I would become a much happier young man. He meant well, but his pep talk had little effect on me at that time. It took a few more years, but I eventually became a big sports fan and a better athlete.

After about a week of camp I called my mother from the telephone near the cafeteria. I cried and I begged her to come get me and bring me home. She tried to calm me down, eventually hanging up on me. Later on I was called into the office of Mr. Katz, who was some kind of psychological camp counselor. He told me he spoke with my mom and they both decided it was best for me to stay at camp and adjust as best I could. Upon leaving his office I decided to escape from camp! I went through the woods towards the main road, thinking maybe I could hitch a ride home. Instead I ended up at a garbage dump. One of the sanitation workers drove me back to the camp. After that I gave up on any future escape plans.

A few days later my parents came up for visitor's day. I showed them around my bunk and the grounds, and again begged them to take me back home. We met with

Mr. Katz, and again it was decided that it was best that I stay on at camp. I'll never forget seeing my parents driving out the main entrance, as I ran after their car, screaming and crying. I now felt even more alone and abandoned. A week or so later camp ended, and I was back home, feeling safe and secure.

Despite being eleven, I was not emotionally ready to be separated from my parents for that amount of time. They thought they were doing what was best for me, but they were wrong. They should have come and got me when I first called. Additionally, camp was only three weeks long! I wish I had the wisdom and maturity to just sit back and enjoy the kids and activities, knowing I'd be back home very soon. That summer at Wel-Met was to be my one and only sleepaway camp experience.

FALL – 1965

In September 1965 I started sixth grade, class 6-3. My teacher was Rosemary O'Connor, a middle-aged, redheaded woman. As she came into the classroom that first day she wandered over to the plants on the window sill, admiring them. Upon watching her I sensed that she was a kind and thoughtful teacher. Although she was easy-going, she was tough when she had to be, and I respected her. I also started my fourth year of Hebrew

School and for the second time had Mr. Diskind as my teacher.

The fall of '65 provided me with some new TV shows to watch, such as the classic Don Adams spy comedy "Get Smart," as well as "Hullabaloo." "Hullabaloo," along with "Shindig," were rock-and-roll variety programs high-lighting performances by current acts like The Beach Boys, The Supremes, The Righteous Brothers, Sonny & Cher, and The Rolling Stones. My favorite new show was "Lost in Space," the science-fiction adventure series about the stranded Robinson family, the Robot, and the evil Dr. Smith. Most episodes were rather campy and childish, but I loved the show anyway. Mark loved the show too as we always discussed the episodes the next day in class. We wanted to be friends with Billy Mumy, who played Will Robinson, as he was the same age as we were.

As I was beginning to outgrow cartoons and children's programs, there were still some new children's shows I enjoyed. New cartoon shows included superheroes like "The Mighty Hercules," "Gigantor," "Eighth Man," and "Astro-Boy." There was also "Speed Racer," "Magilla Gorilla," and "Peter Potamus." Renowned ventriloquist Paul Winchell had a new kid's show called "Winchell Mahoney Time," featuring dummies Jerry Mahoney and Knucklehead Smiff. Other children's programs included "Birthday House," "Beachcomber Bill," and "The Merry Mailman" starring Ray Heatherton, who sang "I'm a Little Teapot" on each show.

In the late afternoon of November 9, 1965, I was sitting in Hebrew class, taking a history test. Suddenly the lights started flickering, then went completely out. As it was already getting dark outside, Mr. Diskind dismissed the class. Walking home I noticed all the street lights were out, as well as lights in all the windows. A blackout had occurred, as a disruption of electricity affected most of the northeastern states and part of Canada. I spent the next few hours with Marvin, walking around with flashlights and putting candles around the hallways and staircases of the Dover B-Wing. My biggest disappointment was that I was unable to watch "The Red Skelton Show," my favorite Tuesday night program. By the next morning power was restored, and the blackout became the main topic of conversation in class.

As 1965 was coming to a close I saw a few more movies. My dad and I went to see the new Bond movie, "Thunderball," as well as the mystery thriller "Ten Little Indians," seen at the Alan Theater in New Hyde Park. I went with my whole family to see the year's biggest blockbuster, "The Sound of Music," seen on a big screen, possibly in Syosset. I'm never ashamed to admit that "The Sound of Music" is one of my all-time favorite films. Although it won the Academy Award for Best Picture, some critics panned the film as being cloying and schmaltzy. I love the story and the music, and I try to watch it whenever it airs on TV. I still get emotional hearing songs like "Edelweiss" and "Sixteen Going on Seventeen."

WINTER – 1966

As 1966 began and I turned twelve, I finally got my own bedroom. I kept the small bedroom while Richie and Randy shared the large one. My parents now slept on the fold-out couch in the living room. As we were growing up and getting bigger our apartment was starting to feel a little cramped. My parents discussed buying a house, and they actually checked out a couple of homes for sale in Queens and Nassau County. Ultimately no move was made, and our current living arrangement stayed as is for the time being.

As sixth grade continued with our usual lessons, some culture entered into our classroom from time to time as it did in prior grades. Our teachers played us some classical records, including Tchaikovsky's "The Nutcracker Suite." One day fellow classmate Richard Rand played his clarinet for us, and on another occasion fellow student Eileen Newman demonstrated an exotic dance.

On Tuesdays and Fridays we attended assembly in the auditorium. Tuesdays were casual, as we were shown a nature film or a film about agriculture and farming. We were repeatedly shown a very cute animated film of a Public Service Announcement with the advisement, "Don't cross the street in the middle of the block." Sometimes we had lectures or discussions, as when one day representatives of the Hopi Indian Tribe came in to discuss their culture and customs.

Fridays were more formal: boys had to wear white shirts and ties, and girls had to wear dresses. Friday's assembly began with the "Color Guard," as five students marched onto the stage with the middle student carrying the American Flag. They were accompanied by patriotic music, like "The American Patrol." We recited the "Pledge of Allegiance," followed by singing either "My Country Tis of Thee," "The Star-Spangled Banner," or "America the Beautiful."

The leader of the assembly was Mrs. Labita, a fifth-grade teacher. She played piano and led the assembly in many sing-alongs, mostly patriotic songs and showtunes. I remember her leading us in tunes like "No Man is an Island," "Our Country's Anthem," "This is My Country," "You'll Never Walk Alone," "My Favorite Things," "Oh, What a Beautiful Morning," "I Believe," "Finiculi Finicula," and "The Happy Wanderer" ("Valderi, Valdera"). During the holidays we sang Christmas songs, even though our Hebrew teachers advised us not to. Although students were always required to sing along, I chose not to participate. Besides being introverted, I didn't think I had a good singing voice and wished to confine my singing to my home. One day during the singing of "76 Trombones" Miss O'Connor came right up to my face to make sure I was singing. As I respected her and didn't want any trouble, I sang along that one time.

Halfway through sixth grade our Principal, Mrs. Lutz, retired. The new Principal was Mr. Max Teufel. We held a ceremony in assembly, honoring her and her long service to the school. She became very emotional as she was presented with gifts, and we sang a song written especially for her, using the same melody as "I've Been Working on the Railroad" ("Mrs. Lutz we really love you, and we hate to see you go").

I was now twelve years old, and my relationships with my sixth-grade classmates had both positives and negatives. Arlene Miller was a tall girl who had acne and who had a crush on Steve Boone of the group The Lovin' Spoonful. She had a little crush on me as well. I didn't find her attractive, but I did touch her breast once in class. I was more attracted to Roberta Rothbard, a pretty brunette who lived in Cunningham Heights. I carried her books home from school a couple of times. Roberta was good friends with another classmate, Jeanette Monard. Jeanette was petite and very cute, and I rode my bicycle past her house in Queens Village a couple of times hoping to catch a glimpse of her.

On the negative side, my need for attention was still strong and sometimes irrational and, unfortunately, I continued teasing and making fun of classmates. Most of the teasing was harmless, like saying to Jean Ho, "Ho Ho Ho." Richard Fitzpatrick, who sat next to me in class, had one ear that was a little pointed and misshapen. I teased him about it, often saying "Fitz's Ear" to him. One day Miss O'Connor took me aside. She told me that

Richard was deaf in that ear, and she would appreciate me not teasing him anymore. I had been unaware of his partial deafness, and I felt ashamed and embarrassed. I never teased him again.

Our school began a charity drive, where we sold boxes of candy to friends and neighbors, with the proceeds going to charity. The boxes contained chocolate nuggets with caramel and were called "Polydoodles." Similarly, in Hebrew School we started collecting money for charity, a charity drive known as "Tag Day." My participation in both charity drives was minimal.

Looking back at the home front, I was fortunate enough to have known one of my great-grandparents, the mother of my maternal grandfather, whom we called "Bubbie." At the time I thought it to be her real name, rather than an informal Jewish word for grandmother. Her real first name was Rose and her maiden name was Rappaport. She had emigrated from Russia and was a very sweet, kind lady who, like my grandparents, spoke both English and Yiddish fluently. We visited her several times in nursing homes in Brooklyn, and I was saddened when she passed away in 1966, well into her nineties.

ASTRONOMY

Beginning in early childhood I was fascinated by the field of astronomy. I read books and purchased some star maps showing the constellations. At night I often looked up at the sky as I tried identifying as many constellations as I can. I also enjoyed reading about the ancient mythology surrounding them. The Hayden Planetarium in New York City had a phone number which I called weekly. A recorded message gave information as to where and when Mercury, Venus, Mars, Jupiter, and Saturn would be visible, as well as the moon and artificial satellites. My dad bought me a small refracting telescope, later replaced by a larger reflecting one. I spent many evenings looking through the telescopes, keeping a journal of my sightings.

For a period of time in the mid-sixties my dad took us to the Hayden Planetarium whenever a new sky show debuted, usually every few months. I was always excited to visit there, with the sky shows, the meteorites on display, and the gift shop. As you walked around the first-floor perimeter, it felt like you were walking through space, as the corridors were darkened and lined with pictures of celestial objects.

My dad always encouraged me in pursuing my passion for astronomy. Whenever there was a special celestial event, such as a lunar eclipse, meteor shower, or a passing comet, he would wake me up during the night. We'd quietly leave our apartment and go up the staircase and onto the roof. Being above the lampposts we were able to observe objects under darkened skies. On a few nights we went up to Cunningham Park to look at the stars. There were often several cars in the parking lot, and I figured other people were there to look at the heavens as well. Little did I know at the time that we were in an area commonly referred to as "lover's lane!" Hopefully our presence there didn't cause much disruption in their activities.

By the sixth grade I was coming home for lunch every day. It was nice having the comfort of my mom in the middle of a school day, even for a brief time. One day after lunch, as I was leaving my building to go back to school, my mom shouted down to me from the kitchen window and told me I forgot my keys. She threw the keys out the window and they landed in some thick bushes. As I went into the bushes to retrieve them, a thorn became embedded in my knee. My mom quickly came down and took me to the doctor in the Cumberland. The doctor numbed my knee and removed the thorn. Afterwards, my mom went with me to school and explained to Miss O'Connor the reason for my lateness. My teacher was understanding, but I wish my mom had let me stay home that afternoon.

Around this time period another mishap occurred. Mark and I were having a fistfight in front of our building, one of many fights we had over the years. Mark had me pinned to the ground. A little girl in my building named Eileen was watching and rooting for me. She picked up a rock and threw it at Mark's head. Mark ducked his head and the rock hit me square in the jaw.

My mouth swelled up and started bleeding, and one of my front teeth became chipped. The nerve going to that tooth was permanently deadened. I went on for many years with a chipped front tooth, finally getting a dental implant many years later.

Unrelated to my chipped tooth, my dentist told me that I needed braces. Apparently my many years of sucking my thumb caused my front teeth to protrude a little and become a little crooked. I went to two orthodontists, Dr. Hershel and Dr. Blumenthal, who both practiced at the Medical Building next to Jamaica Hospital. Fortunately, I did not require the full braces. Rather, I just needed what was called a retainer: one metal bar over my top front teeth and one behind my front bottom teeth, secured by two small rubber bands. The braces seemed to do their job, and they were removed after about a year. Several of my friends and classmates had braces as well, many of them more elaborate than mine. I remember some of my classmates in Hebrew School taking the rubber bands out of their mouths and shooting them at each other!

BOY SCOUTS

Because I was shy and introverted I hadn't been involved in any social organizations like the Cub Scouts or Webelos, as many of my friends were. However, now that I was twelve I wanted to become more outgoing and extroverted. Along with Mark's encouragement, I pushed myself to be more social as I joined the Boy Scouts. Boy Scout Troop 402 met in the social room of the Greenwood, directly across the street from the Dover. Mr. Herman of the Fairmont was the troop leader, and there were three patrols: the Aces, the Gladiators, and the Demons. I was in the Aces, along with Mark Levine, Richard Rand, Steve Porti, Mike Herman (the troop leader's son), Dale Nussdorf (there's that name again), and a couple of others. Our patrol leader was Jerry Benson, the older brother of my Hebrew School classmate Jeffrey Benson. I invited Marvin to come to the first meeting with me. I remember him accidently knocking over a mirror, then running out, ending his brief Boy Scout career (typical Marvin.)

I found the Boy Scouts rewarding and educational, as it improved my social skills and helped with my personal growth. My patrol went on a couple of 5-mile hikes around Queens. We memorized the Boy Scout Motto and Slogan, and we learned Morse Code, how to tie different knots, how to administer first aid, and how to read maps. We also learned about citizenship and comradeship. We did some arm-wrestling, and Mr. Herman came up with some crazy competitions like who can hold their breath the longest. Each meeting began with the Pledge of Allegiance and ended with us crossing our arms, holding hands, and singing "Taps" (Day is

Done.) I also subscribed to the Boy Scout monthly magazine, "Boy's Life." I read the Boy Scout Handbook from beginning to end, and I received a Merit Badge in Astronomy.

My life with the Boy Scouts included two overnight trips. The first trip, in the winter of 1966 or 1967, was to Alpine Scout Camp in Alpine, New Jersey. Several fathers volunteered to escort us to the camp as we carpooled. The weekend was very down-to-earth and rugged as we slept in cabins in the woods with no heat or electricity, save for the fireplace. I slept in a top bunk, with Mark sleeping underneath me. We cooked our meals over an open fire and ate using our mess kits or vittle kits. The highlight of the weekend was earning our "Totin' Chip" card, by learning and practicing the proper handling, care, and use of knives, axes, hatchets, and saws. My dad recalls me coming home covered in dirt (after all, how can a normal active boy ever enjoy himself without coming home dirty, right?) Overall, this trip was a pretty fun experience.

The second trip came a few months later as we went to another Boy Scout camp in New Jersey. This time we really got to experience camping as we pitched tents and slept in sleeping bags. We went on some hikes in the woods, armed with a compass, a contour map, and a "survival kit" which was basically a "Band-Aid" box containing bouillon cubes, water purifier tablets, matches, a fish hook, antiseptic, and bandages. Some hikes required us to bring along a canteen and a knapsack on our back, which made hiking more challenging. We witnessed an Indian war dance around a bonfire, roasted marshmallows, and had a game of egg-toss, where I splattered portly co-leader Ronnie Freed's hands with eggs.

All our supplies, including camping equipment, were purchased at Wilson's, a popular scouting supply store on Jamaica Avenue in Queens Village.

With the Boy Scouts I only reached the rank of Tenderfoot. I completed all the requirements to move up in rank to Second Class when our troop disbanded, probably due to financial reasons. I was very sorry to see my troop disband, and I tried to find another troop to join. I went to a meeting of another troop at a church in Queens Village, but as I didn't know any of the other scouts there, I decided not to join. I look back at my Boy Scout experience with fondness.

SPRING – 1966

As I didn't know how to swim as well as I wanted to, my parents decided to send me for lessons. On several consecutive Saturday mornings my dad drove me to the Hotel Paris in Manhattan where I took swimming and diving lessons. I did indeed learn how to swim better, but after experiencing a belly-flop I gave up learning how to dive. With summer just around the corner the lessons turned out to be a worthwhile venture.

As I said, I was a "mama's boy," and up to age twelve did not show much interest in sports or social activities. As they turned eleven or twelve, most boys from Hilltop joined the Little League. Most of my friends joined, including Mark, Eddie, Marvin, and Eli. Although I wanted to be with my friends I felt I was a poor athlete and was not interested in playing baseball. Nevertheless, I did enjoy watching the Little League Parade, as one Saturday morning every May they marched up 204th Street. As I looked out my bedroom window, I watched each team marching their way up to the Little League fields, accompanied by marching bands. It was all pretty exciting.

As springtime continued, and I was becoming a little more sociable, I began to further enjoy the outdoor activities Hilltop had to offer. We all got excited as we heard the bells of the Good Humor truck as it rambled onto 204th Street. My mom would wrap up change, then throw it out the window to me and my brothers. Harry was our Good Humor man; he always had his white uniform on with the silver coin changer hanging from his belt. We watched with eager anticipation as Harry reached deep into the back freezer or side freezer to get us our treats. I usually bought a "chocolate burst," vanilla ice cream with chocolate and nuts in a waffle cone. We loved ringing the bells, but Harry did get annoyed if we honked the horn. Mister Softee and

Bungalow Bar trucks also made their way down the street. There was also a truck called "Chow-Chow Cup" selling Chinese food. Their most popular item was chicken chow mein served in a cup made out of Chinese noodles.

There were three kiddie rides mounted on top of flatbed trucks coming down 204th Street every spring and summer: a small Ferris wheel, a large swing with several rows of seats, and a whip. I could see the rides from my bedroom window, and whenever I heard the trucks and the kids outside, I ran down hoping to catch them before they left.

My friends and I discovered a lot of new games to play in front of the Dover. Kids from other buildings joined with us to play "May I Take a Giant Step?" and "Red Light Green Light 1-2-3." We played box ball using a pink-colored rubber ball, either a Spaldeen or a Pensie Pinkee. There was three-box, five-box, and two-box, aka "Hit the Penny." One day some of my friends became a little enterprising: Eddie set up a roulette wheel in front of the Dover and, hoping to drum up business, he continually shouted out "Roulette! Play Roulette!" Mark set up a table next to him as he tried selling some used books and comic books. Richie and Randy briefly got into the business scene as well, walking around the neighborhood selling unwrapped cookies.

We also spent a lot of time in the Dover playground, playing punch ball, kick ball, handball, and a game with a large rubber ball called "spud." On many occasions of punch ball, when throwing home we'd lose the ball as it went sailing over the short fence and down Francis Lewis Boulevard. The owner of the ball always yelled "chips," so that he'd be reimbursed for the loss of his ball. I also recall one evening when my dad invited my friends up to our apartment to play "Johnny-on-the-Pony." Despite my mom's disapproval we had a lot of fun leap-frogging and jumping on top of each other.

I also started riding my bicycle a lot. I got rid of my green, 24-inch two-wheeler and bought a 26-inch red Pierce-Arrow. I often rode up Francis Lewis Boulevard, then turned left onto Epsom Course, then left again onto Dunton Avenue. That area just west of Hilltop was known as Jamaica Estates or Terrace Heights and was made up of private homes. There was a small hospital in that area called Terrace Heights Hospital, where my mom once spent a few days having a procedure done. There was also a small wooded area near Pompeii Avenue called "Cannon Hill." Sometimes I rode my bike there and hung out with the kids from that neighborhood. Riding south on Dunton Avenue over to 197th Street was a very steep hill known as "Suicide Hill." We had to be very careful riding down that hill, as I remember Sammy falling off his bike there and getting his head a little bloody. Sammy was the last of my friends to learn how to ride a two-wheeler without training wheels, and I give credit to Eddie, who spent many days patiently teaching him how to ride.

Stickball was becoming very popular among Hilltoppers. We usually played "Fungo," where in lieu of a pitcher the batter would throw the ball up to himself, then try to hit it. Most of the time we played on 204th Street, but on occasion we played in the parking lot behind the Dover. There was an ornery man named Mr. Raddish, who lived in the B-Wing and whose window faced the parking lot. He always yelled out the window to us, something like, "Get out of the parking lot, ya rotten kids!" As we were not a threat to him we usually ignored him and he eventually left us alone. When we opted to play stickball using a pitcher, we either went to the south side of the Greenwood or the side of Bohack, where there were walls to throw the balls against. The walls were also used for games of handball.

When the weather was nice, weekends and afternoons after school provided a lot of fun times. Whenever I left my apartment there were always kids outside, playing games, eating ice cream, or just hanging out. Even the private policemen in Hilltop hung out and socialized with us. However, although I was becoming more outgoing and sociable, I still wish I wasn't still shy and depressed, as I could have enjoyed myself a lot more.

Mr. Paxson, my fifth-grade teacher, ran an after-school program in the hot-lunch room, where students played games like Chinese checkers, bumper-pool, nok-hockey, and pinball. While I didn't spend much time there, Richie and Randy enjoyed the games and activities. My mom or I often went down to the school in the late afternoon to pick my brothers up and take them back home.

By this time Salvatore's Restaurant got some new competition as Gaby's Pizza opened in our strip mall near Bohack. On the day of their grand opening I went there during lunchtime, along with some of my classmates. The place was packed as they gave away free pizza and soda. Gaby's also had a jukebox in the back, and I enjoyed playing three songs for a quarter.

Sometimes on my way home from school my friends and I stopped at Goodies, Kirsans, or some other store in the strip mall to get candy, bubble gum, or school supplies. Situated between Goodies and Joe's Barber Shop was an entrance to a staircase going up to some offices, followed by two double doors leading onto Foothill Avenue. As this route provided a shortcut to go home, we frequently tried taking it. A janitor or maintenance worker, whom we called "Onion Head," always chased us back down the staircase. If we were lucky we could sneak past him and take this short cut home.

June of 1966 arrived as I graduated sixth grade. We had a graduation ceremony in the auditorium, where Mrs. Labita led us in singing a graduation song with words set to her favorite tune, "The Happy Wanderer." We signed autograph books in the school yard and said our goodbyes. Classmates wrote a lot of silly poetry in those books. For instance, Margarita Morolla wrote, "If Arlene Miller lived across the sea, what a fast swimmer Robert would be." We wished each other goodbye and good luck, as we knew we wouldn't see all of our friends and classmates in the Fall: some students were going to Junior High School 109 in Queens Village, while others were going to Linden Junior High School 192 in St. Albans.

SUMMER – 1966

As the summer arrived I breathed a great sigh of relief as I found out my parents would not be sending me back to sleepaway camp. As Richie and Randy returned to Cross-Island Day Camp, I attended another local day camp, this one located at the Samuel Fields YMHA in Little Neck. This year of camp was known as a pre-teen, or "tween" camp. Mondays, Wednesdays, and Fridays were spent at the Henry Kauffman Campgrounds located in Wheatley Heights, Suffolk County, Long Island. Tuesdays and Thursdays were spent taking various day trips. Additionally, to the best of my recollection, in July we took a two-day overnight trip to Amish Country in Pennsylvania where we slept in a large barn, and in August we had an overnight camping trip in Brewster, Putnam County, N.Y.

Each morning of camp I carried with me a duffle bag containing my bathing suit, towel, and change of clothing. My mom gave me a brown paper bag packed with a sandwich, a piece of fruit, and Scotch ice to keep things cold. She included a small can of fruit juice, either Motts AM or Motts PM. On the mornings of our days at Henry Kauffmann's, the camp bus let us off at the base of the campgrounds. From there we hiked up a long, steep, dirt hill, to one of several small shelters in the woods. We put our stuff in outside cubbyholes, then proceeded onto our activities. The activities were very similar to those at View Hill Day Camp: Arts and Crafts, volleyball, handball, badminton, archery, hiking, and scavenger hunts, with swimming and softball after lunch. As I enjoyed climbing trees, I often opted to sit on a tree branch and watch some of the activities, rather than participate in them.

I was more excited about camp when we went on our various day trips. Those trips included Rockland Lake State Park, the Bronx Zoo, Catskill Game Farm, Rye Playland, Sterling Forest, Westbury Music Fair, the Statue of Liberty, and a Kibbutz in New Jersey. One day we went to the Stratford Theatre in Stratford, Connecticut, to see a version of Shakespeare's "Falstaff." The play almost put me to sleep.

I also recall a trip to Sagamore Hill, former home of President Theodore Roosevelt. I enjoyed seeing the grounds and the historic buildings, but I was taken aback when I saw heads of lions, tigers, and rhinos mounted on the wall. I asked a fellow camper, "why would a great man like a President of the United States want to kill such magnificent animals?" My fellow camper didn't understand it either.

My favorite trip was going to Bear Mountain via the Hudson River Day Line. The ship left from Manhattan, then went up the Hudson River, underneath the George Washington and Tappan-Zee bridges, and over to Bear Mountain State Park where it left us off before continuing its journey up to West Point. While at Bear Mountain we visited a very nice little zoo, followed by swimming in a huge public swimming pool. The camp bus brought us back home.

We made trips to various beaches, including Rockaway Beach, Sunken Meadow, and of course, Jones Beach. While at Jones Beach we swam in the large saltwater pool at the West Bathhouse. We went into the pool with a locker room key tied around our wrist. Girls were required to wear bathing caps, and of course we had the "buddy system" in place for all swimming activities. I remember the water being very cold, and by the time I got used to it the whistle was blown and it was time to leave.

During every camp season my "fun-in-the-sun" was somewhat spoiled by the sunburns I got every year from those day trips to the beach. I also received numerous mosquito bites which my grandmother, as well as

Sammy's mother Ida, said were due to mosquitos liking me because I had sweet skin.

On the bus rides back to the Samuel Fields Y we were serenaded by the girl campers in the back. They sang and clapped along to current hit records, including "Hanky Panky," "The Birds and the Bees," "Little Red Riding Hood," "The Pied Piper," "See You in September," and "Sealed with a Kiss." They loved singing the song by The Cyrkle, "Red Rubber Ball," which I also frequently sang at home and in the car. Their favorite song was The Rolling Stones' "(I Can't Get No) Satisfaction," as they giggled when singing, "I can't get no girl reactions." While I enjoyed their singing, I was usually able to lean my head against my duffle bag and take a little nap.

Obviously, there were those occasional days of inclement weather. With whatever day camp I attended, whenever it rained we usually stayed inside the building or casino and watched the movie "The Wizard of Oz." "The Wizard of Oz" is obviously an all-time classic, and I always watched its annual airings on television. That being said, I wish they occasionally opted to show some other films as well.

I have a vague recollection of experiencing a very special, pleasant summer day in 1966. I think it took place sometime in late August. It was a very warm, hazy late afternoon as my family and I went upstate to attend some sort of outdoor festival or carnival. There were various rides, attractions, and food vendors, along with bleachers on either side. There was also a Drive-in movie theater nearby. A big orange full moon had just come up over the horizon, and I recall hearing the Jonathan King song, "Everyone's Gone to the Moon" over the loudspeaker. I sat in the bleachers as I watched various circus-type acts. My parents bought us ice cream and other treats. In my mind it was a perfect day, encapsulated in time.

FALL 1966 – WINTER 1967

September 1966 had arrived. Although it was back to school, this year would be different. For the first time in seven years me and my fellow Hilltoppers would be attending a new school, Linden Junior High School 192 in St. Albans, Queens. P.S. 135 graduates from Queens Village would be going to Junior High School 109 which was closer to Hilltop than Linden.

In order to promote integration in Public Schools the New York City Board of Education was in the process of "busing," whereby white students would be sent to schools based on the percentage of minorities there rather than based on the school's proximity to the student's home. Therefore, us white Hilltoppers were sent to Linden, which at the time was 85% black. I had no issues with attending Linden. All my friends from Hilltop would be going there, many of them in the same classes as mine. In addition, most of my friends, as well as myself, were put into "Special Progress Enrichment," or "SP/SPE" classes. These were three classes for students who had high grades in elementary school. I was in class 7SPE1. All my friends were in the "SP/SPE" classes except for Gary Fishman and Marvin Berk, who had been left back for a second time. Also, since Linden was two miles away we were no longer able to walk to school. The school bus picked us up every morning in front of the Hampshire.

We started our first day by going to the school cafeteria and filling out Delaney cards, used to take attendance in each class. We then had lockers assigned to us. The combination to my lock was "23-2-10," which fellow Hilltopper Andy Menkes, aka "motor-mouth," blurted out to everybody. I then met my homeroom teacher, Howard Mandell. Mr. Mandell was a big, husky, thirtyish guy who had a girlfriend on the faculty, Miss Moskowitz. He was also my Social Studies teacher. I was sorry to see Mr. Mandell leave as the following year he resigned to become a Police Officer.

I had Mrs. Peterson for typing, Mrs. Lovette for English, Mrs. Somers for Math, Mr. Beauchamp for Spanish, and Mr. Weiner for Science. We also had the option of taking either music or shop. Most of us Hilltoppers chose music. I requested the clarinet but Mr. Block, my music teacher, assigned me the alto-saxophone. I had to bring my instrument to school every Tuesday and Friday. My case was rather small, and I felt

127

bad for Mark Levine, who was assigned the cello. He had to lug it to school twice-per-week, and it was almost as big as he was!

As we began Junior High one of the first things instilled in us was school spirit. We were given a welcoming speech from the Principal, Mr. Oxenhorn, and we learned and memorized our school song:

"O Hail Linden Junior High

As the Years Go by We'll Be True

We'll Pause in Our Future Ways

To Remember Days Spent with You

O Hail to the Green and White

And Our Future Bright Filled with Memories

Our Thoughts and Our Loyalty

Shall Belong O Linden to Thee"

In addition to Junior High I began my fifth and final year of Hebrew School, again with Mr. Lazar. As I said previously, the fifth year of Hebrew School was when we all turned thirteen and had our Bar-Mitzvahs. Many students, including myself, quit Hebrew School right

128

around their Bar-Mitzvah date. I attended Hebrew Class from September to December. Concurrently I took private Bar-Mitzvah lessons from Rabbi Brenner in his office, and I also had Alan Tannenbaum of the Ivy Ridge tutor me once a week in my apartment. My Bar-Mitzvah was scheduled for January 28, 1967. The reception was to be held at the Hillside House on Hillside Avenue, the same catering hall where I recently attended Eddie and Sammy's receptions. My parents were very excited knowing their first-born son was about to have a Bar-Mitzvah, and my mom started writing out the invitations.

As I was adjusting to seventh grade and attending Hebrew School and Bar-Mitzvah lessons, I was hit with devastating news: my mother had been diagnosed with breast cancer. During the course of the last several months my father had been taking her to various doctors. When first told of her condition my father decided not to tell my brothers and I as he did not want to worry us and have it adversely affect our schoolwork. He just kept telling us she'd get better. What hit me hard was one day in the fall of '66 when an ambulance arrived in front of our building and the medical staff took my mother out of our apartment on a gurney. We were very scared, but my mother just smiled up at us and told us not to worry. She came home later that day, but a few days later she was admitted to Long Island Jewish Hospital in New Hyde Park.

129

Despite my father's and grandparent's assurances I knew my mom's health was seriously declining. I went many times to the hospital with my father, brothers, and grandparents. At that time the hospital had a ridiculous policy that minors were not permitted to visit patients, even family members! My father and grandparents took turns visiting my mom while my brothers and I hung out outside the hospital. There was one day in late December when my grandfather snuck me in to see her. She was going in and out of consciousness, but she did smile up at me as if to assure me that everything would be OK. This was the last time I was to ever see her. The doctor had told my father that my mother's cancer had spread to her lymph nodes, and that he should start gathering family members together. Even after receiving this horrific news, my dad was still telling us that she would be OK and would be coming home soon.

January 5, 1967 was a very sad day for me and my family and one I remember vividly. It was a clear, cold Thursday afternoon as I got off the school bus and went into my apartment. My dad opened the door, and he and my grandparents had tears in their eyes. My grandmother told me that my mother "passed away." I was in immediate shock as I sat down at the dining room table. Seeing my dad and grandparents crying I felt a tear go down my cheek. I was obviously shocked since I had been holding out hope that she would get better. Sadly, she had passed away at only 35-years-old.

As is traditional in the Jewish faith the newly-deceased is buried as soon as is practical. My dad told me the funeral would be tomorrow, Friday. I naturally assumed I would be attending the funeral, but my dad said my brothers and I will be going to school as if it were just another day. I thought this to be a very poor decision on my father's part. I don't think a child should suddenly lose a parent, then pretend like nothing happened. My dad consulted with my grandparents and they decided the best thing for us was to keep our usual daily routine. Looking back, I think they regretted not having us attend the funeral. Early that evening Richie and Randy got home and my dad told them the sad news. I remember Richie crying, as well as being surprised at not going to the funeral. One year later we were finally able to say our proper goodbyes as we all went to Beth-Moses Cemetery in Elmont to attend my mom's unveiling. The temple's new rabbi, Rabbi Richtman, presided over the ceremony.

That Friday morning I went to school still in a state of shock. My dad or grandmother apparently notified the school because Mr. Mandell and Mrs. Lovette, as well as classmates, expressed their sincere condolences to me during those respective classes.

The next several days were spent sitting Shiva, the Jewish tradition where friends and family gather together to mourn the loss of a loved one. Many of my aunts, uncles, and cousins gathered at my house, bringing with them cakes and other pastries. Friends and neighbors were being especially kind to us. I remember Marvin and Sammy offering to play Monopoly with me. Later on Mark and Eddie asked me to play Monopoly with them, but I chose to play with Marvin and Sammy since they asked me first. Everyone was very kind and sympathetic to me and my family. When Richie and I had to visit Dr. Spellman in the Cumberland he was overly kind and let me play with one of his instruments. As he was one of my mom's doctors, maybe he felt some guilt or responsibility.

Due of my mother's death my Bar-Mitzvah reception was cancelled. However, the actual Bar-Mitzvah recital at the synagogue went on as scheduled. I shared the stage with Randy Gelb, who lived in the Belmont and was in some of my classes at P.S. 135. The Bar-Mitzvah recital went well as I was told I only made one mistake. Following the recital we all went to my Aunt Dinah's house in Port Washington where we ordered in pizza. My grandparents presented me with a wristwatch as a Bar-Mitzvah gift. Because of my mom's recent death the whole day was kind of low-key and bittersweet.

A few weeks later I attended Eli Fishman's Bar-Mitzvah reception at the Hillside House. This became memorable because I got into a fistfight with Eli during the reception! (I had a lot of fistfights with Eli and Mark during those years).

February had arrived and we were coping with my mom's death as best we could. My grandmother often came over to help with the cooking and cleaning. My dad hired a middle-aged black woman named Pauline to come in once a week to clean. She worked for us for a few weeks, but my dad decided he wanted someone who can be with us on a more full-time basis. He hired a woman named Betty, a tall, middle-aged, plain-looking woman with a German accent. She came to our apartment in the morning, cooked, cleaned, went grocery-shopping, then went home at the end of the day. My brothers and I never took a liking to her; she was stern, stuffy, and seemed to lack a sense of humor. We often gave her a hard time, calling her "Beauty Betty." She used to call us "clowns." She worked for us for about a year, after which my grandmother took over most of the cooking and cleaning duties.

PUBERTY

Around this time, early 1967, I began going through that confusing phase of boyhood known as puberty. As with any normal thirteen-year-old, new thoughts and emotions started to enter my consciousness. My hormones started going a little out-of-whack and physical changes to my body were taking place. Marvin got hold of issues of Playboy Magazine which he passed around to me and Sammy. We also took turns reading a library book titled "How Babies Are Born." There was some sexual ambivalence as I found myself being attracted to both boys and girls. Many kids in school and in Hilltop started looking physically appealing to me. While I know that this ambivalence can be a normal part of puberty, I may have exceeded normalcy in my relationship with Marvin Berk.

Around this time Marvin and I started an intimate relationship, something Marvin first called "doing sexy," later calling it "playing pussy." We went into the Dover bicycle room or the laundry room bathroom and had "close encounters." I will spare the details other than to say it was a bit more than hugging and kissing. Sometimes Marvin called me on the telephone and said something like, "Hey Robbie, my mother and sister are out. You want to come up and play pussy?" Sometimes we did it in my bedroom when no one else was home. On nice days we went into the bushes behind the Fairmont. Other times we went over to the woods in Cunningham Park. While at the park we often spied on couples who were "making out." Marvin liked to collect used condoms, which we referred to as "scum-bags." One day he collected a bunch of condoms in the woods, then threw them through an open window of a moving bus on Francis Lewis Boulevard! We were both discreet and told no one about our encounters.

I also became a bit of a voyeur as I watched Marvin and an unnamed male friend fool around a couple of times. One day in the bicycle room I watched Marvin "feel up" Mary Brockway, a young blond girl who lived across the street. The encounters between Marvin and I continued for about two years; after that we both seemed to outgrow this phase and continued our friendship platonically.

I also had physical relations with Mark Levine, although less intense. We felt each other up a couple of times, once in my apartment, once in his. I recall one day fooling around with Mark in his apartment when his mother suddenly walked in. As we quickly pulled up our pants my zipper got stuck! It was a little embarrassing. Once I went into the laundry room bathroom of the Ivy Ridge as Eli Fishman, Michael Jaffe, and I exposed ourselves. As I turned fifteen, any sexual ambiguity I had seemed to disappear. From then on my sexual focus was confined to the fairer sex.

SPRING – 1967

As the spring of 1967 began and I concentrated on schoolwork and recovering from my mom's death, I took comfort in my favorite TV programs. The 1966-1967 TV season included some new shows which became favorites of mine. Monday nights on channel 4 "The Monkees" debuted and quickly became very popular with my brothers and I. Tuesday and Wednesday nights had "Batman," starring Adam West.

135

My brothers loved it and I watched it even though I found it campy and silly. Thursday nights saw the debut of the original "Star Trek," and Friday nights I watched "The Time Tunnel." My favorite show at the time was probably "The Avengers," the British Spy Drama starring Patrick MacNee as John Steed and Diana Rigg as Emma Peel. I watched it on Friday nights with my dad, who kept telling me how good Mrs. Peel looks. We were both upset when Diana Rigg left the show the following season.

Around this time I saw several motion pictures, including the thriller "Blindfold," starring Rock Hudson, "Fantastic Voyage," "The Fortune Cookie," "Cast a Giant Shadow," "Barefoot in the Park," "Grand Prix," "How to Succeed in Business Without Really Trying," "Born Free," the James Bond spy-spoof "Casino Royale," and "Follow Me Boys," a nice movie about the Boy Scouts starring Fred MacMurray. I also saw "You Only Live Twice," the first James Bond movie seen with friends rather than with my dad.

In the spring of '67 I went ice-skating for the first time. I went with a group of friends and neighbors to Skateland in New Hyde Park. I fondly remember Jeffrey Weiss and a friend of his holding my hand and helping me skate. I recall hearing the Turtles' new record "Happy Together" during the commute there, and it was a very pleasant day for me. Also that spring, Mr. Mandell took our Social Studies class on a bus trip to Washington, D.C. It was my first visit to our Nation's Capital, and it was fun and educational.

There's nothing positive about losing a mother at a young age. That being said, up to this point I was a "mama's boy." I had been very close to my mom and showed little interest in playing sports or watching sporting events. As I was no longer able to cling to my mom, I started becoming more outgoing and sociable as I got into playing stickball, softball, and basketball with my brothers and friends. As spring went into summer I found myself spending more and more time outdoors, hanging out with friends while Betty and my grandmother continued taking care of the household. I started following Major League Baseball and became a big New York Mets fan, especially enjoying the heroics of their great rookie pitcher, Tom Seaver.

In May I attended Marvin Berk's Bar-Mitzvah, held in the Dover social room. The room was very small; I guess his parents couldn't afford a more lavish affair. The month of May also brought the annual Science Fair to school. For my project my dad helped me build a computer. It was very simple as it demonstrated electric currents and circuitry.

Summer was approaching, and in order to bring back some normalcy and maybe some culture into our lives my dad took my brothers and I to a pop/classical concert held at the bandshell in Forest Lake State Park. I remember not enjoying the concert very much as I preferred the more contemporary music of the Beatles and the Monkees.

My dad took us along on many errands, whether it was clothes shopping, to the car wash, or to lunch at a local diner. With my mom's death fresh on our minds I really felt bad for my father. I remember seeing his eyes get red, especially when certain songs came on the radio, such as "What Now My Love (Now That You Left Me,)" and "(If It Takes Forever) I Will Wait for You." It was a sad time for all of us but my dad was holding up pretty well.

Despite my father's sadness and suffering he tried to maintain a cheery disposition as often as possible. Each morning he woke us out of bed with a smile and a song:

"Good Morning to You, Good Morning to You,
We're All in our Places, With Sun-Shiny Faces."

His cheerfulness helped my brothers and I get through some very painful and challenging times.

SUMMER – 1967

The summer of '67 arrived, affectionately known as "The Summer of Love." Richie and Randy again attended Cross-Island Day Camp, and I attended the Samuel Fields YMHA for the second year. I was looking forward to this year being better than last year for two reasons: while the year before we went on trips two times a week, we now would be going three times weekly, only going to Henry Kaufmann Campgrounds on Tuesdays and Thursdays. Also, my friend Sammy Gische was to be in my group this summer. Sammy and I took different buses, however. Sammy's bus driver was named Trudy, mine was named Dotty, with a third driver named Kitty.

My summer with Sammy was contentious at times. I think he was looking for attention as he teased me a lot and carried the "Booga" moniker into our group, resulting in some kids and even counselors calling me by that name (they misspelled it as "Bugah"). I had to shove Sammy to the ground a couple of times to shut him up! Aside from my issues with Sammy, the summer was fun. In July we went on a three-day, two-night trip to Cape Cod, where we went on a nature hike. I remember seeing the play "The Odd Couple," starring Henry Morgan and Jesse White, at the Cape Playhouse. The August three-day trip saw us going upstate, where we saw Hal Holbrook doing his famous portrayal of Mark Twain at the Saratoga Performing Arts Center ("Mark Twain Tonight!")

That summer had me listening to some new records, both at camp and on my father's car radio. Songs like "I

Think We're Alone Now," "Carrie-Anne," "Up, Up and Away," the Jefferson Airplane's "Somebody to Love," and the Monkees' "Pleasant Valley Sunday."

One trip I remember well was going to Lincoln Center to see a live performance of "South Pacific," starring Florence Henderson. Around intermission time I was brought into the security office because a security camera caught me using a can-opener to scratch-up a bathroom door! Another of my mis-guided attempts to get attention.

Camp ended with the counselors giving out special awards to each camper. I was given an award for tree-climbing, given my inclination to climb trees at the campgrounds.

FALL – 1967

As the Fall of 1967 began, the kids from the apartment directly below us, Helene and Jeffrey, moved away with their parents. Moving into their apartment were the Siegels. Jay and Brian Siegel were about the same ages as Richie and Randy and they became friends.

I began eighth grade, class 8SPE2. Although I continued taking the school bus, I occasionally took public transportation. I would walk down the hill to Hillside Avenue, then take the Q77 bus to Hollis Avenue where Linden was located. I had Mrs. Rader for homeroom and English, Mr. Feinstein for Math, Mr. Raizen for Social Studies, and continued with Mr. Beauchamp and Mr. Weiner for Spanish and Science, respectively. My music teacher was Mr. Sheppard, who was soon replaced by Mr. Seiden. I liked Mr. Seiden because he once gave Mark and I a ride home.

By the eighth grade I had made some new friends from class. There were classmates from St. Albans, Springfield Gardens, and Cambria Heights who did not attend P.S. 135, but whom I got to know well. There was Mark Danish and Wayne Shepherd, Robin Seligman and Susan Grossman, Glen Beecher and Michael Mantlo, Charles Malley and Joseph Barczuk (who was very strange), and James Krauss and Beau Braun. There was Karl Delaney, who was very tall and had acne. I used to tease him, calling him "Doofy Delaney." I'm surprised he never kicked my butt for teasing him; he probably should have.

There was a black kid named Kevin Wallace whom I first met when we were in Washington, D.C. the previous semester. He was very friendly with me and Mark Levine, but he teased us a lot as well. Kevin, who played the French Horn, had a certain routine with me in music class. Before each class he'd steal a book or something else of mine, then I'd chase him around the hallways and staircases. It was good exercise and my relationship with Kevin was always good-natured. I liked music class and I especially remember fellow Hilltopper and bandmate Eddie Ruben playing the song "Windy" on his saxophone.

Suffice it to say, there were a lot of interesting personalities and routines that were part of life at Linden. There was something known as "operation sweep." Sometime during class a P.A. announcement was made, stating "this is operation sweep." At that time any student found wandering the hallways would be sent to the Principal's office for disciplinary action.

Lunchtime was also interesting. Mr. Radin and Mr. Block (not the music teacher) would stand in front of the lunchroom. Mr. Block would shout, "Stop Ya Tockin', Stop Ya Tockin'" until things quieted down. One time Mark Levine and I were playing pat-a-cake, causing Mr. Radin to scream at us, "Hey Pat-a-Cake Nuts!" Once things got quieter they called each table one at a time to come up and get their meals. The lunches often included meatball heroes and Sloppy Joes. Scooter Pies were the preferred dessert. (the nutritional guidelines as set by current Boards of Education were nowhere to be seen). During lunchtime fights frequently broke-out. All the students stood up to watch. I also used to stand and start screaming, just to get some attention.

I regret to admit that I still felt a great need for attention, and as a result I sometimes behaved immaturely and inappropriately. I often teased students as I did in elementary school. I recall once teasing fellow

142

classmate Lisa Atwell in the lunchroom. She became so angry she threw her plate of food in my face! I just stood there and smiled, but believe me, I was totally embarrassed.

I also learned the art of throwing spitballs. Mark Levine, Kevin, myself, and some other students were throwing them, sometimes at the girls, sometimes at each other. There was a black girl in our class named Diane Watson. We didn't like her as she was loud, nasty, and rude. She became a frequent target of our spitballs. One day I was told to report to the Dean's office. The Dean, Mr. Adler, said that Diane lodged a complaint against me for throwing spitballs, which I confessed to. He then said he would call my home and speak to my mother about this (not knowing my mom had recently passed away.) My grandmother answered the phone. That evening I was mildly reprimanded by my father and grandmother. I never threw spitballs at her again, but I also felt like a scapegoat. (Why did she only tell on me?) Mark and Kevin stopped throwing spitballs at her as well, for fear of repercussions.

I wished I had been assertive in a more positive and effective way. One day in Mr. Feinstein's Math class Billy Toles, sitting behind me, kept poking me with some kind of TV aerial, causing me to squirm and fidget. He was being encouraged to continue this by Mark Levine and Kevin. Mr. Feinstein kept telling me to sit still, unaware as to why I was fidgeting. I didn't tell him what was happening. I should have told the teacher what was going on, or better yet, yanked the aerial away from Billy. As I said, I wished I had handled some situations better, with more assertiveness and more maturity.

In addition to our more cerebral classes, Physical Education was stressed as well. Mr. Racanelli and Mr. Trell were our gym teachers. We did a lot of calisthenics, played dodgeball, and did some rope climbing (I almost got to the top). We also played some basketball as we practiced shooting baskets and lay-ups. I still considered myself a poor athlete, and I hated it when Mark Levine laughed hysterically as I missed shot after shot.

In the fall of '67 the Holliswood Jewish Center began a "youth group" where teens and pre-teens of both sexes could play games and socialize. We met there on weekend afternoons. The temple provided us with bagels and cream cheese as we played bumper-pool, nok-hockey, and checkers. The Beatles' "Sgt. Pepper's Lonely Hearts Club Band" was the #1 album in the country at that time, and our youth group played that record over and over. As I was becoming more attracted to girls I especially liked looking at some of the young ladies in the group, like Judy Redler and Sandra Siegel.

As 1967 drew to a close I saw the movie "To Sir, With Love," starring Sidney Poitier, at the Drake Theatre on Woodhaven Boulevard. I also recall attending Mark Levine's Bar-Mitzvah reception, held at Leonard's of Great Neck, a very popular and opulent catering hall.

WINTER – 1968

The year 1968 began as I found myself getting more into music, in particular top-40 radio. My dad used to wake me up on school mornings around 7am. While we were both busy getting dressed and ready to go to school and work, he listened to his portable transistor radio. He either had on Big Wilson on WNBC or "Rambling with Gambling" on WOR. Those two stations provided a nice mix of news, sports, weather, and an occasional oldie song. However, I wanted to listen to other stations with music I could call my own.

At that time New York City had two major top-40 Pop Stations aimed at teens and pre-teens, WMCA and WABC. WMCA had disc jockeys who were known as the "Good Guys." The station was famous for its yellow "Good Guy" sweat shirts, which were worn by many teenagers. WABC's disc jockeys were known as the "All-Americans." I bought my own little transistor radio and became an avid listener of WABC. The weekday disc jockeys were Harry Harrison, Ron Lundy, Dan Ingram, Bruce Morrow (aka "Cousin Brucie"), and Chuck Leonard. On Tuesday evenings I'd put aside my homework for a few hours and listen to Cousin Brucie's countdown of the top records of the week. I had a yellow wall clock in my room, and what I did was write down the top twelve songs on small pieces of paper, then tape them to the corresponding numbers on the clock. I would make changes to the clock's numbers every week so they would match the countdown numbers for that particular week. I fondly remember some of those records from early '68, which included "Daydream Believer," "Hello-Goodbye," "Green Tambourine," "Bend Me, Shape Me," "Woman Woman," and "Judy in Disguise (With Glasses)."

I came to love what became known as "bubble-gum music," those simple pop songs contrived and marketed to appeal to pre-teenagers; songs like "Simon Says," "1-2-3 Red Light," and "Yummy Yummy Yummy." There was a store in Jamaica called Tri-Boro Records. Whenever Mark, Eli, or I heard a new song we really liked we hopped on the bus to Jamaica to purchase those singles. I remember going to Mark's apartment to listen to "Reflections" by Diana Ross & the Supremes, then going over to Eli's to play "Snoopy vs. the Red Baron" by The Royal Guardsmen, then shooting over to my place to listen to "Valleri" by The Monkees. I began what soon became a very extensive collection of 45RPM records. I always considered 1968 to be one of the best years for music.

Besides being involved in top-40 radio, I also got into buying and reading comic books, especially those of superheroes. My favorite comics books included Superman, Batman, Spiderman, Daredevil, and X-Men. I also read comic strips from the newspapers, which were affectionately known as "the funnies."

SPRING – 1968

By the spring of '68 my father had joined Parents Without Partners, a social organization for singled, widowed, and divorced parents. He attended meetings regularly and began dating, usually going out on Saturday nights. As I was now fourteen years old, I no longer required a baby-sitter. My dad would go out, leaving me to watch over Richie and Randy. On his nights out my brothers and I really enjoyed our new unsupervised freedom. We played football in our living room using a throw pillow as a football, me vs. Richie and Randy. Jay Siegel, living directly below us, used to recall how his ceiling would shake, rattle, and roll as we were tackling each other. We always had our new living-room color TV set turned on, and we'd take breaks from playing football to watch our favorite Saturday evening shows, which included "Get Smart," "My Three Sons," and "Mannix." I fondly remember those unsupervised evenings.

After being on the dating scene for a few months my father settled on one woman. Her name was Ellen Gottlieb. She looked like a schoolteacher, late 30's with glasses. She lived in a two-bedroom apartment in Flushing with her son Ricky. Ricky was about five or six-years old, and I don't recall much about him other than he liked to hang out in his underwear. My dad frequently took us to Ellen's apartment, usually Saturday or Sunday afternoons. We'd have dinner there or sometimes we'd all go shopping or out to lunch. To be honest, my brothers and I didn't like her very much; not because she was a potential replacement for our mom, but rather because she was kind of stern and stand-offish. I don't recall her ever asking us about school, friends, or anything else in our personal lives.

Sometime in the late spring we went with Ellen and Ricky upstate, first to Albany and then to a bungalow colony. There were a lot of bugs around and I didn't enjoy myself. Soon after that we went with them on a weekend trip to Philadelphia. We saw the Phillies play the Mets at the old Connie Mack Stadium. As a Mets' fan I found this outing much more enjoyable.

As I continued through eighth grade I went on three school trips to Manhattan to see movies. First we went to see the movie, "Camelot" starring Richard Harris. Another time we went to see the re-release of the classic "Gone with the Wind," which I had never seen before. The most memorable of these trips came in April. Mr. Weiner, our science teacher, told us he's taking the class to see a new science-fiction movie called, "2001: A Space Odyssey." He said he was really looking forward to it as the advanced press spoke very highly of the film and its ground-breaking special effects. I saw the film and was mesmerized by it. Like many viewers I found the film's meaning difficult to understand and open to many interpretations. Mr. Weiner spent the entire next class discussing the film. Fellow Hilltopper and classmate

Barry Steinberg made the point that the onboard computer was named HAL, because the letters "H," "A," and "L" were all one letter before "I," "B," and "M" in the alphabet. A few days later I bought and read the book the movie was based on, authored by Arthur C. Clarke.

Mr. Weiner always had interesting classes. He had us read the best-selling paperback "Silent Spring" by Rachel Carson, which dealt with the adverse effects of DDT and other pesticides on the environment. One weekend Mark and I went over to Mr. Weiner's house in Fresh Meadows to say hello. We didn't get to see him as his wife said he was taking a shower. The next day in class Mr. Weiner politely requested us not to come to his house again without an invitation.

As mentioned before, I had a lifelong interest in astronomy and visited the Hayden Planetarium many times during childhood. To further enrich my knowledge and appreciation of this subject my father enrolled me in three courses held at the planetarium, beginning in the fall of '67 and continuing through June 1968. The courses were, "Astronomy for Young People," "Special Topics in Astronomy for Young People," and "Advanced Topics in Astronomy for Young People." Each course lasted several weeks and were held Saturday mornings in basement classrooms. On some Saturdays we drove to the elevated #7 train station at Bliss Street in Woodside. From there we took two trains to the planetarium. My father and brothers would hang out while I was in class, then we'd return to Queens. Other times we drove directly to the planetarium. My dad and brothers threw around a football while I attended class.

Coming back from the planetarium we stopped at various diners in Queens for brunch. I usually had eggs or pancakes, and we enjoyed playing songs on the jukebox, located at each booth (just like at Gaby's, three songs for a quarter). We played many of the same songs every time we ate at a diner, especially "Winchester Cathedral," "Born Free," "Downtown," "Moon River," "Strangers in the Night," and songs by Herb Alpert & the Tijuana Brass.

There was a fast-food joint on Queens Boulevard called "Burger & Shake." We often stopped there as we were coming back from the planetarium or when visiting Ellen and Ricky. I always enjoyed eating there, and upon our arrival I showed off my usual childish behavior as I'd sing a made-up song, "I Want a Thick Vanilla Milkshake."

One time at a diner on Queens Boulevard we ran into Mrs. Somers, my seventh-grade math teacher, who was eating with her family. For some reason I became really intimidated, but we went over to say hello anyway. Mrs. Somers was probably my least favorite teacher, as she came across as stern, nasty, and cynical. One example was with Jeffrey Elias, a fellow classmate who lived in the Hampshire and was cousins with fellow

Hilltopper Mindy Wach. Jeffrey was very tall and spoke with a speech impediment. Mrs. Somers once told him in front of the class that with his mumbling he'd probably be best suited to drop out of school and go fight in Viet-Nam. I don't think she was a very nice woman.

Despite the lost of my mom and my negative feelings towards Ellen, my depression was lifting. With my astronomy classes, dining out, and my increased involvement in music and sports, 1968 was becoming much more satisfying than the previous year. I now found myself less interested in staying home watching TV, more interested in being outdoors, playing ball, and going to ballgames. Ellen bought me a musical instrument called a Melodica. I played tunes on it for hours and hours, and as of this writing, I still have it!

On April 4, 1968 tragedy struck the country as civil-rights leader Martin Luther King, Jr. was assassinated. Although this was a nationwide tragedy it affected Linden especially hard as most of the student body was black. There was a big memorial ceremony in the auditorium, and they even considered re-naming the school after Dr. King. Up to now the black girls often bothered the white boys from the SP/SPE classes. They stuck us with compasses or they bent bobby-pins and snapped them on our butts, causing pain. Some male black students shoved us around from time to time as well. Following Dr. King's assassination these incidences increased. Some students felt this was in retribution, since he was killed by a white man. It was unfortunate for me, as all I wanted to do is get from class-to-class without harassment. These incidences continued on-and-off through the ninth grade.

Sadly, only two months later Senator Robert Kennedy was assassinated while campaigning in California to be the Democratic Nominee for President. These assassinations, along with the escalating Viet-Nam War and the contentious Presidential campaign, were a reminder what a tragic and tumultuous year this was for our nation.

As eighth grade was winding down the annual science fair was back. For my project my dad helped me make a display showing how solar energy works. We made a collage of pictures and articles, and did a demonstration using a high-intensity light and a solar cell.

As spring turned into summer I found myself spending a lot of time outdoors with friends, playing stickball in the street and softball in the park. I also rode my bicycle a lot, sometimes with friends, sometimes alone. I rode through Cunningham Park and explored various dirt roads and side roads in Fresh Meadows and Jamaica Estates. My bike had no gears, so it was very good exercise. I remember one day riding to Kissena Park in Flushing, along with Mark, Eddie, Marvin, Stevie, and Woody. We raced around a bike track and had a nice time. Afterwards my stomach was feeling a little queasy. I bought a roll of Tums ("Tums for the

Tummy"), and I wound up eating the whole roll. When I got home and told my grandmother that I ate a whole roll of antacids, she panicked and called the Poison Control Center! They told her that Tums is very mild and assured her there was nothing to worry about. My grandparents cared about me and were sometimes over-protective, but I always appreciated their concern.

SUMMER – 1968

The summer of 1968 arrived as I began my final year as a camper. Instead of the Samuel Fields Y, I went to the Flushing YMHA Day Camp (I'm not sure why the change was made). Each morning I walked across Francis Lewis Boulevard and waited for the Q76 bus, along with Randy Gelb and Gloria Ginsburg (Sammy's cousin). I got off at Union Turnpike, then waited for the camp bus to pick me up (Randy and Gloria went their separate ways). The camp bus would rendezvous with the other buses at the ballfields in Fresh Meadows, then we'd go on our respective trips My bus counselor's name was Bonnie. At the end of each day my dad picked me up at Union Turnpike and drove me home. Sometimes I walked home from Union Turnpike if I wasn't too tired.

The camp routine was the same as at Samuel Fields: two days at the campgrounds, three times a week, day trips. The day trips were familiar: The Day Line to Bear Mountain, horseback-riding, Jones Beach, Rye Playland, etc. For the July three-day overnight trip I returned to Washington, D.C., where we did a photo-op with NYS Congressman Seymour Halpern. For the August three-day trip we went to upstate New York, visiting Howe Caverns and other attractions. We saw a summer-stock version of "Oliver!," and we spent one night sleeping in the dorms in Oneonta and the other night sleeping outdoors in sleeping bags at some campground. There always seems to be one bad apple to spoil the fun: there was a nasty kid named Murray who constantly picked on me, poking me, calling me names. He even made fun of how I ate an ice cream sandwich! He had a buddy named Kenny, who occasionally picked on me as well (calling me "Retardo,") but he was more stupid than mean.

As I went through my days in camp I carried my little transistor radio with me, fixed onto WABC. Some of the new records that summer included "Soul-Stoned Picnic," "Lady Willpower," "This Guy's in Love with You," "Hello, I Love You," and the Rascals' "People Got to be Free." The girls on the back of the bus continued serenading us, adding some new songs to their repertoire, especially the song "Reach Out in the Darkness" ("I think it's so groovy now, that people are finally getting together"). As the summer came to an end, so did my life as a camper.

One day near the end of August I was hanging out on the swings in the Dover playground. Eli came in with his radio and told me about this new Beatles record that WABC kept playing over and over. A few minutes later "Hey Jude" came on the radio. We both loved the record and a few days later we went to Jamaica to purchase "Hey Jude" b/w "Revolution."

FALL – 1968

September 1968 arrived, and I was ready to begin ninth grade when…a teacher's strike began! New York City schools would be shut down for two months as a confrontation began between the Central School Board and the United Federation of Teachers, led by Albert Shanker. The strike involved some teachers from Ocean Hill/Brownsville in Brooklyn who were dismissed amid charges of anti-Semitism and racism. When the strike began no one knew how long it would last; therefore, some parents began looking elsewhere for their kids to attend classes in the interim. For a couple of weeks Marvin's sister Linda drove Marvin and I to some church or community building in Bayside to attend classes. Every evening I watched the news for updates on the strike, hoping it would end soon. I was more comfortable at Linden and I felt bad for the teachers and students. The strike finally ended November 17, as the

Central School Board capitulated and re-instated the teachers.

I began ninth grade, class 9SPE2. My classmates were identical to last year except the homerooms were split up. For instance, I had my old math teacher, mean old Mrs. Somers, for homeroom, while Mark Levine had Mr. Franks. I again had Mr. Raizen for Social Studies. I also had Mrs. Cooper for Art, Mr. Hershkowitz for Earth Science, and Mr. Mason for Spanish. I had Mr. Winkler for Hygiene, a class that only lasted two months as Mr. Winkler departed the school.

I'm embarrassed to admit this, but through the eighth grade I was still occasionally sucking my thumb in class. I had never really felt ashamed about it until the eighth grade, when I became more interested in the opposite sex. I remember Robin Seligman giggling at me as I was sitting there, thumb-sucking. I recall sitting next to fellow Hilltopper Reva Ross in Spanish class, wondering what she must think of me: a fourteen-year-old who sucks his thumb in public! As I entered ninth grade and became more attracted to girls, I wanted them to be attracted to me as well. Therefore, on the first day of ninth grade I made a vow to myself that I would never again suck my thumb in class or in public, and I never did again!

As I wanted to be more appealing to girls, just as they were to me, I started taking more interest in dressing well and being well-groomed. Early at my time at Linden

156

boys were required to wear ties. A girl running for Student President promised that if elected she would do away with this requirement. She was indeed elected, and the tie requirement was abolished. Despite this I still occasionally wore a tie. I tried approving my physical appearance. My hair was getting longer, and I applied Top-Brass hair gel to it. Every morning I took extra care in making sure my nails were clean and my hair was well-combed. The rest of the fall semester went well, with only minor confrontations in the hallways and lunchroom.

The year 1968 was big politically: it was a Presidential Election year, and there was unrest at the Democratic Convention with anti-war protesters. Earlier in the year President Johnson announced he will not be seeking re-election. Vice President Hubert Humphrey won the Democratic nomination and was up against Republican nominee Richard Nixon, with Alabama Governor George Wallace as the Independent Party nominee. My family and I strongly supported Mr. Humphrey, especially because of his opposition to the Viet-Nam War. We were obviously disappointed when Nixon defeated Humphrey in a very close election.

Around this time my father and Ellen decided to go their separate ways. My dad began dating again, mostly on Saturday nights, and my brothers and I resumed our living-room football heroics.

The fall of '68 brought with it some new TV programs. On Monday nights channel 4 aired "Rowan & Martin's Laugh-In," which actually debuted earlier in the year. My brothers and I loved this show, with its irreverent humor and fast-paced jokes. Plus, I enjoyed seeing Goldie Hawn and Judy Carne dancing around in bikinis! Some of the other new shows included "Mayberry RFD," "Here's Lucy," and "Julia." I also went to the movies. Eli and I took the Q36 bus to the Queens Theater to see the original "Planet of the Apes," starring Charlton Heston. Other movies seen included "The Producers," "Ice Station Zebra," and the Beatles' animated "Yellow Submarine."

The year 1968 was the first year I really followed professional football passionately. I purchased some plastic miniature goal posts as well as miniature helmets representing all NFL and AFL teams. What I did was mount the helmets on the goal posts in the order corresponding to the teams' place in the standings. As the standings changed from week-to-week I re-positioned the helmets accordingly. At the time I was more of a N.Y. Jets fan than a Giants fan, mainly because of quarterback Joe Namath. Namath, with his swagger, flamboyance, and his ability to lead the team to eleven regular-season wins, quickly became a football hero of mine. When playing football in the living room I pretended to be Jets' running back Matt Snell or Emerson Boozer. When playing in the street I pretended I was George Sauer or Don Maynard catching passes from Broadway Joe.

I played a lot a touch football in front of my building on 204th Street. As Sammy couldn't run very fast he usually played quarterback. He had a good arm but often threw the ball behind us, prompting us to shout out what became a Hilltop catch-phrase: "Wrong Side, Gische!"

Mark often played quarterback as well. Others who sometimes joined in included Marvin, Eli, Eddie, Woody, Arthur Tanney, and Andy Menkes. Sometimes older guys joined in, like Bobby Gelfand, who was a nice guy, and Bruce Markowitz, who wasn't so nice and used to shake our hand and then squeeze it as hard as he could. There was also a 300-lb. guy named Foreman, who was a jerk.

Sometimes I played a little too passionately. Once I ripped my pants and scraped my knee diving on the concrete while trying to stop Eddie from scoring a touchdown. Another time while running to catch a ball, I ran into a double-parked car, causing bruises to some private areas.

In addition to the games on 204th Street, we sometimes rode our bikes to either Cunningham Park or the- little-league fields, where we got into pick-up games. We mostly played touch but occasionally played tackle. I thought I was a pretty good receiver and I actually had thoughts of playing professionally someday, not an uncommon dream for a fourteen-year-old boy.

I pasted a large picture of Joe Namath on my bedroom wall, surrounding it with smaller pictures of pro football receivers like Lance Alworth and Otis Taylor. I also started following professional basketball. Although I rooted for the New York Knicks, I put up pictures of L.A. Lakers stars Wilt Chamberlin, Elgin Baylor, and Jerry West.

In late '68 Marvin gave me a pink-colored plastic speaker. I attached it to my transistor radio and put the speaker on my headboard. I was now able to lie in bed and listen to music with much higher quality sound and clarity. I spent many nights enjoying the music.

As 1968 was coming to a close I was very sorry to hear that my friends Eddie and Stevie Wolkis will be moving out of Hilltop as their parents bought a house in Plainview, Long Island. I knew Eddie since we were little, and as I said, he was the only friend from Hilltop who never teased me or belittled me. He was also probably the most intelligent out of all of us.

I look back at 1968 with fondness. Certainly I was still grieving over the loss of my mother; that loss you never completely get over. But the year saw me becoming a little more assertive and outgoing, maybe a little more mature. As I continued pursuing my interests in astronomy, sports, and music, and with more interaction with friends and neighbors, things were going well.

WINTER – 1969

As 1969 began WABC had a new #1 record, "I Heard it Through the Grapevine" by Marvin Gaye, and the country got a new leader as Richard Nixon was sworn in as our 37th President, with Spiro Agnew sworn in as Vice President. Then on January 12th I got to watch Superbowl III as the Jets upset the heavily favored Baltimore Colts, 16-7. My friends, brothers, and I were ecstatic. Joe Namath really put his money where his mouth is as he had guaranteed a Jets victory. An exciting end to the football season. Three days later I quietly celebrated my fifteenth birthday.

The winter of '69 was cold and snowy. In particular, a February snowstorm blanketed the northeast and mid-Atlantic states with New York City getting about 20 inches of snow. The storm became known as "Lindsay's Snowstorm," as Mayor Lindsay was criticized for not responding to the storm adequately. Schools were closed for several days, which didn't bother me. I remember climbing mountains of snow on Foothill Avenue and having many snowball fights.

By now Eli was my best friend, more so than Mark or Marvin. Although we were good friends there was something in our relationship that often resulted in fistfights, just like at his Bar-Mitzvah reception. Eli was often loud and irritating, which bothered me. Every morning at the bus stop Eli and I would start a fistfight. Fellow Hilltopper Andrew Bagon refereed the fights. Bagon, always an annoying and immature guy, referred to our fights as "Booga vs. Egghead." ("Egghead" being one of Eli's nicknames). The fights were pretty innocuous as we rarely landed a punch.

Eli and I went bowling together, usually at either Cardinal Lanes or Hollis Lanes, both of which were located on Jamaica Avenue. We ate out a lot, and took many subway rides into Manhattan. We went to TV tapings of the original "Match Game" with Gene Rayburn and the original "Jeopardy" hosted by Art Fleming. We also saw a taping of comedienne Joan Rivers new talk show, "That Show with Joan Rivers," with guest Godfrey Cambridge.

One day we took the bus to Elmont to a place called Wal-Cliffe. Wal-Cliffe had a roller-skating rink in the winter and a swimming pool in the summer. On our way back I recall waiting for the bus on Hempstead Turnpike during a downpour, and I recall some guy coming up to me and pinching me in the face for no apparent reason!

As March of '69 began our music class began graduation rehearsals. The two songs we practiced over and over were "Pomp & Circumstance" and "Love is Blue." By the time graduation came we were all sick and tired of those two songs.

The rest of the semester was going well. I particularly remember one day in Mr. Raizen's Social Studies class as he was teaching us about the planets. I was always quiet in class, never raising my hand for fear of embarrassment. However, because of my interest in astronomy I actually volunteered to teach part of the class! Mr. Raizen had slides of the sun, moon, and planets. I went to the front of the class to explain each slide. When discussing the planet Venus, I told the class that there was a belief at the time that Venus had bodies of water on its surface. I then went to the next slide and, lo and behold, it showed bodies of water on it. My credibility among my classmates was secure.

SPRING – 1969

I had a really enjoyable day on April 5th of 1969. Eli and I went into Manhattan to see the annual New York Auto Show, held at the old New York Coliseum at Columbus Circle. I wasn't into cars and I was not an auto-racing fan; nevertheless, it was fun seeing all the new cars, especially the foreign ones. We got patches from Renault, Fiat, Datsun, and others, and put them all over our jackets. We got to meet professional race-car drivers Dan Gurney and Cale Yarborough, as well as Olympic skier Jean-Claude Kiley. We also met O.J. Simpson. Simpson was the reigning Heisman Trophy winner out of the University of Southern California, and he was about to begin his pro football career with the Buffalo Bills. We got his autograph and he later spoke to us. He was standing in the doorway to some back room and he told us he wanted a hot-dog. (Maybe if we got him a hotdog his post-football career would have taken a different turn!)

One weekend in the spring my dad took my brothers and I for a weekend upstate at the Nemerson Hotel in South Fallsburg, N.Y. (I think it was a Parents Without Partners sponsored weekend). I remember watching my dad play basketball, and we saw a show starring nightclub comedian Gene Baylos. My dad introduced us to a woman he'd apparently been dating awhile, Roberta Blackman. She seemed pleasant and I got better vibes than I did with his previous girlfriend Ellen. Roberta was widowed with three sons who were with her on the weekend, Larry, Stephen, and Jonathan, ranging in age from 12 down to 5. Little did I know how serious my dad and Roberta's relationship would become; I would find out in a few more months. The weekend went well as I kept my radio to my ear, listening to new songs like "Proud Mary," "Aquarius/Let the Sunshine In," "Hair" by the Cowsills, and the Beach Boys' "I Can Hear Music" (which I thought was called "Ike and His Music.")

My dad's Aunt Hattie and Uncle Al lived in Jamaica, not far from my grandparents. Uncle Al worked at Bonds Clothing Store and was friends with Jack Lang, sportswriter for the Long Island Press. Through Mr.

164

Lang he was able to secure two season tickets to the New York Mets which he gave to me! (what better year to have season tickets than in 1969 when the Mets went on to become World Series Champions!) Eli and I went to opening day, and to about a dozen other Met games that year. We got autographs from Ed Kranepool and Jerry Grote. We got to see a lot of Seaver, Koosman, Agee, Cleon Jones, Harrelson, Swoboda, and the other Mets. Eli was also a Baltimore Orioles fan and loved Brooks Robinson. We went to some Yankee games when the Orioles were in town. Eli rooted for Baltimore, I rooted for the Yankees.

On June 8th Mark Levine and I went to Mickey Mantle Day at Yankee Stadium. Mantle had retired a year earlier, and this was a day to honor his legacy and retire his #7. It was a great day for both fans and players as we all paid tribute to this Yankee legend.

The spring of '69 continued as I again started riding my bicycle a lot, mostly by myself. I explored several neighborhoods of eastern Queens and rode several times on the old Long Island Motor Parkway, an abandoned and mostly demolished road from the early 1900's. The original highway had extended from Queens out to Lake Ronkonkoma, and a small segment still remained intact, extending from Francis Lewis Boulevard to Commonwealth Boulevard and Alley Pond Park. It was very pleasant riding along this road in the spring, listening to the birds and watching the leaves and flowers grow. The warmth of the spring, the smell of the flowers, and the new songs on the radio helped further lift my depression.

My Earth Science teacher was Mr. Hershkowitz, a likeable but quirky guy who I used to make fun of, as he was always rubbing his hands together, and would repeatedly say "as such" and "Okay, now." He took us on a couple of very enjoyable trips. One was to the Museum of Natural History, which I had already been to many times. I mostly hung out there with Mark Levine and Andy Menkes, frequently comparing Mark to the apes and baboons on display there. Another trip was to the Palisades in New Jersey, just south of the now-defunct Palisades Amusement Park, where we studied and collected rock samples to coincide with our geological studies. This outing also became relevant to my ninth-grade science fair project. My dad helped me design a display with pictures of dinosaurs and fossils, along with a display of various rocks. Earth Science had become my favorite subject at Linden.

As June was arriving my classmates and I were getting ready to graduate from Linden and starting to prepare for high school in the fall. As busing was still the rule in New York City Public Schools, Hilltop students at Linden were scheduled to attend Andrew Jackson High School, a predominantly black school located in Cambria Heights. Many students and their parents were upset, as the parents wanted their kids to attend a high school that was closer to home, and that was also predominantly white, in order to avoid the same racial tensions that occurred at Linden. What many students did was give the schools an address of a friend or relative living outside the busing zone, thereby allowing them to attend the school of their choice. So while most Hilltoppers did indeed enroll in Andrew Jackson, many went to other schools as well, such as Francis Lewis, Martin Van Buren, Benjamin N. Cardozo, and Jamaica High Schools.

Mrs. Rosen, our guidance counselor, told us about Stuyvesant High School, a school in Manhattan specializing in math and science. She said that if we take and pass a certain test administered by that school we can enroll in that school for the Fall. Mark, Eli, myself, and some other students jumped at the chance as we took the test, then waited anxiously for the results. A few weeks later, Mrs. Rosen gathered us in the cafeteria to tell us the results. Mark and Eli jumped around excitedly as they found out they passed, but to my dismay I did not. As I was almost in tears, Mrs. Rosen came over to console me, and told me all is not lost; I can attend summer school and, if I pass, I can enroll at Stuyvesant in the Fall. Summer school classes would be held at Washington Irving High School in Lower Manhattan and would be taught by Stuyvesant faculty members. Although I wanted to enjoy a leisure summer, with the chance to go to Stuyvesant, and be at the same school as Mark and Eli, I eagerly signed up.

One day in June I went to a party at Susan Grossman's house. Susan's brother played in a band, and I listened to him play some current songs, such as the

Beatles' "Get Back" and Donovan's "Atlantis." I played a very "G-rated" spin-the-bottle with Susan, Mark Levine, Mark Danish, Robin Seligman, and Diane Wildow.

Junior High School graduation was held at the Queens Theater in Queens Village. It was presided over by Linden's new Principal, Bernard Fox. Again, I played my saxophone in the band, playing "Pomp and Circumstance," "Love is Blue," and a few other numbers. We wore dark green cap-and-gowns with a gold tassel, and I was pleased that my dad and both grandparents attended. Of course, not having my mom there to see me graduate made the day bittersweet.

SUMMER – 1969

The summer of '69 was here as I began my six-week summer school. Each morning I took the bus to Jamaica, then took two trains into Manhattan. I attended two classes: Math with Mr. Glotzer and English with Mr. Wozniak. Also, on Wednesdays we went up to Midtown for group therapy, which was to help with our transition into high school. I usually got back home by early afternoon, hoping to catch the end of "Jeopardy," which my grandmother would be watching. Sammy often joined us in watching, as he called "The Daily Double," "The Daily Dinkle." My grandmother often prepared

168

lunch for me, as well as for Sammy and Eli, her specialty being salmon croquettes on a bed of lettuce and a glass of milk. Afternoons were often spent playing stickball on 204th Street with Marvin, Sammy, Stephen Daniels, Eli, and his brother, Teddy.

The biggest hit records in the summer of 1969 included "In the Year 2525," "Crystal Blue Persuasion," and the record heard most often during my weeks of summer school, Stevie Wonder's "My Cherie Amour."

Those summer evenings were spent hanging out with my friends and brothers and watching TV with my grandmother. Every weeknight my grandmother and I watched the 10:00 o'clock News on channel 5, hosted by Bill Jorgenson. I ate peanut butter on white bread and watched the somber news at the end of each program as they scrolled down the names of the soldiers killed in Viet-Nam the previous day.

On July 20 a major historic event occurred as Neil Armstrong and Buzz Aldrin became the first men to walk on the moon, fulfilling President Kennedy's goal to put an American on the moon before the end of the decade. I sat in front of the living room TV with my brothers, father, and grandparents, and watched with great awe and excitement. I had been passionately following the U.S. space program since its beginnings, from the Mercury and Gemini projects through the Apollo project. As a big fan of space exploration, I felt exhilarated and inspired.

169

About the same time the moon landing was taking place, my personal life was about to have a major upheaval. My dad came to me with the news that he and Roberta were getting married! Not only that, but he and Roberta just bought a house in East Meadow, Long Island, and we would be moving there in September! I think I stood there in shock, with my mouth open for about three days. I was going to leave Hilltop, the only home I've ever known, not to mention leaving all my life-long friends. Plus, I would be living with four new people who were virtual strangers to me.

I was naturally upset with this news, but I had no choice other than to move forward and adjust to my new life as best I could. I had a couple more weeks of summer school, and naturally thought I would stop going at this point; after all, with the move out to Long Island I would be attending a high school out there. I didn't want to continue summer school under false pretenses, but my dad told me to complete both courses as it would be helpful for my education. I adhered to my father's wishes and completed summer school without telling them that I will not be attending Stuyvesant.

August 15, 1969 was an important day for the "younger generation," as it was the first day of a 3-day event in upstate New York known as Woodstock. It was a music festival billed as "three days of peace and music," and was widely regarded as a pivotal moment in popular music history. On the same day Woodstock began my family and I were having their own pivotal moment. On August 15th my dad and Roberta were married in Roberta's parents' house in Howard Beach. It was a simple Jewish ceremony, attended by my brothers, Roberta's sons, and her parents, Harry and Yetta Silver. Later that day my dad and Roberta left for their honeymoon in Atlantic City. Unfortunately, when they returned, my dad discovered his car had been stolen, our 1962 gold Chevy. He figured some hippies must have stolen it to "go up the country" to Woodstock.

The last two weeks of August were very difficult for me, as I told all my friends and neighbors the news. At the time I had a tape recorder and several reel-to-reel tapes with recordings of me, my parents, grandparents, and my brothers. Some recordings went back many years. In a moment of anger and emotion over moving out of Hilltop I tossed my tape recorder and all the tapes into the garbage bin in the basement. One of the biggest regrets in my life was not holding on to those tapes and the memories attached to them, especially the audio of my mother.

My dad said that our new house would not be ready for moving into until late September. So I would not miss the beginning of tenth grade he said I will spend the first few weeks of that month living with my Aunt Shirley, Uncle Meyer, their daughter Phyllis, and her sons, Bruce and Steven. It was convenient as they lived in East Meadow only a few blocks away from our new home. As I knew them all fairly well, I was okay with it. My dad said I had to choose between the two high schools in the area: East Meadow High School or Tresper Clark High School. Since I didn't know a single student from either school it really didn't matter to me. I chose to attend East Meadow High School, maybe because it was easier to spell.

It was one night in late August or early September, a few days before moving out of Hilltop. I stood alone in the Dover playground for a long time, looking up at the moon and the stars. I felt apprehensive, nervous, and very alone, as I tried to contemplate what my new life would be like. I just hoped and prayed that my future would be ok; this moment in my life is what I consider the end of my childhood and the end of the first chapter of my life story.

CONCLUSION

Looking back at my childhood and my life in Hilltop, I see it as a mixed bag of both positives and negatives. The negatives were of course headlined by the death of my mom, along with my depression and behavioral issues, the bullying, my jealousies, and the physical punishments. But there were also many positives: the great music, movies, and TV shows I experienced, the joys of the holidays, the fun at the bungalow colonies, the pursuit of my interest in astronomy, the many toys

172

and games, the friendships, the love from my parents, grandparents, and brothers, and the warmth and comfort I felt at home with my mom. Those positive memories are the ones I cherish and hope to remember forever.

ABOUT THE AUTHOR

Robert Altman is now happily retired after working for the Nassau County Health Department for thirty-six years. He lives in Florida with his wife of twenty-six years, Michele, and his dog Oliver. His daughter Lindsay continues to reside on Long Island. Rob enjoys golfing, hiking, astronomy, politics, and travelling. His is on a Senior bowling league and is involved with a local Democratic club. He enjoys listening to music of the sixties, as well as TV shows from that era, as it takes him back to an easier and simpler time.

Made in the USA
Monee, IL
01 August 2021